Educators Praise *Third Space*

"*Third Space* is a thrilling book about teaching and learning. It affirms in clear, resonant tones how wondrous schooling can be. *Third Space* demonstrates how important arts education is, particularly to students and teachers in high poverty schools. I recommend *Third Space* not just to educators but to business leaders, policy makers, and to anyone interested in improving the quality of education for all our children."

— MILT GOLDBERG
EXECUTIVE VICE PRESIDENT, RET., NATIONAL ALLIANCE OF BUSINESS
DIRECTOR, *A NATION AT RISK*

"Students across the country are dropping out of school at frightening rates. *Third Space* directly confronts this fundamental challenge: how can we make school a meaningful experience for every student, an experience that engages them deeply in learning and school life, unleashes their capacity to be self directed and innovative, and nurtures their desire to be contributing members of society. *Third Space* provides invaluable lessons to policy makers on how the arts are a way to meet that challenge."

— TOM HOULIHAN
EXECUTIVE DIRECTOR, COUNCIL OF CHIEF STATE SCHOOL OFFICERS

"*Third Space* helps to advance our understanding of how arts education contributes to our determined efforts to provide every student the kind of education that results in content mastery, plus the important capacity to create, to solve problems, and to dream."

— SHARON P. ROBINSON
PRESIDENT AND CEO, AMERICAN ASSOCIATION OF COLLEGES FOR TEACHER EDUCATION

"*Third Space* presents an unusually rich tapestry of effective arts programs in the schools and, equally important, identifies the human resources and administrative systems required to initiate and sustain such vital work."

— GERALD E. SROUFE
    SENIOR ADVISOR, AMERICAN EDUCATIONAL RESEARCH ASSOCIATION

"*Third Space* validates the power of the arts to engage teachers and students in a shared quest for learning. Its research documents how schools have transformed themselves through the arts by creating a context and the motivation for academic success. It is a powerful affirmation for those who believe in the arts and an enticing invitation to those who still need to be convinced."

— JOSEPH VILLANI
    DEPUTY EXECUTIVE DIRECTOR, NATIONAL SCHOOL BOARDS ASSOCIATION

"*Third Space: When Learning Matters* clearly illustrates why it is more important than ever to ensure access to arts education for every student in America, particularly those in high poverty schools. As the research demonstrates, arts education changes schools, changes communities, and most significantly, changes the lives and learning experience of students."

— BRENDA WELBURN
    EXECUTIVE DIRECTOR, NATIONAL ASSOCIATION OF STATE BOARDS OF EDUCATION

"*Third Space* proves that arts education programs enhance student learning, and help to give each student a strong sense of self, increase teacher efficacy and satisfaction, and foster community cohesion and support for the schools. Diverse arts education programs can be an equalizer for low-income students, and a very important component in the equation to close the student achievement gaps that currently exist."

— JOHN I. WILSON
    EXECUTIVE DIRECTOR, NATIONAL EDUCATION ASSOCIATION

THIRD SPACE

when
learning
matters

Lauren M. Stevenson | Richard J. Deasy

ARTS EDUCATION PARTNERSHIP

PUBLICATIONS OF THE ARTS EDUCATION PARTNERSHIP

"You Want to Be A Part of Everything": The Arts, Community, and Learning

The Arts and Education: New Opportunities for Research

Envisioning Arts Assessment

Teaching Partnerships: Report of a National Forum on Partnerships Improving Teaching on the Arts

Critical Links: Learning in the Arts and Student Academic and Social Development

Champions of Change: The Impact of the Arts on Learning

Gaining the Arts Advantage: Lessons from School Districts that Value Education

Learning Partnerships: Improving Learning in Schools with Arts Partners in the Community

Young Children and the Arts: Making Creative Connections

These AEP publications, as well as executive summaries and informational brochures, are available for purchase or download at www.aep-arts.org

---

Cover: The artwork on the cover was adapted from the print, *Frozen*, by Braylan, a student at the Clarkton School of Discovery in Clarkton, North Carolina.

Book Design: Design Nut, LLC, Kensington, Maryland.

Arts
Education
Partnership

Copyright © 2005 by Arts Education Partnership. All rights reserved. Printed in the United States of America. No part if this book can be reproduced in any manner without prior written permission of the Arts Education Partnership.

Partial funding for this book came from a grant from the Department of Education. However, the contents do not necessarily represent the policy of the Department of Education, and you should not assume endorsement by the Federal Government.

For information:
Arts Education Partnership
One Massachusetts Avenue, Suite 700
Washington, DC 20001-1431
202.336.7016
www.aep-arts.org
aep@ccsso.org

ISBN: 1-884037-97-6

Table of Contents

Foreword

"Just read your paper
And you'll see
Just exactly what keeps worryin' me
Yeah, you'll see the world is in an uproar
The danger zone is everywhere"

— RAY CHARLES

The morning of September 11, 2005 was as clear and bright as the one four years ago. The radio news show I was listening to bounced between stories of America's efforts to mark that tragic fourth anniversary and the still emerging stories of tragedy, horror, and racism in the wake of Hurricane Katrina. Two voices kept bouncing around in my head. First was Ray Charles singing, "yeah, you'll see the world is in an uproar/ the danger zone is everywhere." And the second was my own, asking, "Where are all of these children going to go to school?" The next question I asked myself was how their teachers could possibly address the enormous complexity of their new students' reality.

What could make children who had experienced such peril and loss feel that school is a safe haven, not another danger zone? In truth, this question is not only relevant to the schools that have opened their doors to children of New Orleans and the Gulf Coast. It is a question that can be asked of any school, but especially any school whose students are, as we say, on "free or reduced lunch"—in other words, children who live in economic poverty. (I want to be clear that I do not equate economic poverty with cultural, spiritual, relational, moral, intellectual, or aesthetic impoverishment. Qualifying for free or reduced lunch measures family income, not the other qualities mentioned above.)

Indeed, I believe this is the question raised and addressed in the study reported on in this book. Lauren Stevenson and Dick Deasy remind us that creating safe zones where children will feel secure enough to engage in the challenging work of serious learning can be accomplished in high poverty schools. Indeed, they share ten examples that demonstrate this possibility, even as they reveal the complexity of the challenge of doing this. What do these ten schools have in common? In each of them, studying and/or making works of art (paintings, dances, plays, songs, films, and so on) plays a significant role in their curriculum and their culture.

To my mind, Stevenson and Deasy ask many critically important questions. They want to know how schools can become truly powerful learning environments, not simply places that can report increases in test scores – at any cost. They want to understand the importance of situating rigorous teaching and learning in a strong community. And they want insight into what it is about studying and making works of art that creates a special and powerful "third space" between and among teachers, learners, and works of art.

This last question is, I believe, an essential key to understanding how engaging in arts activities can transform students' relationship to their own learning, teachers' ideas about teaching, and the culture of the school. That the arts can catalyze changes in a school that lead to a healthier and more productive environment should not come as a surprise (though it does not seem at all obvious to most people in the field of education). The arts are widely accepted as one of the defining elements of any culture, community, society, or civilization. If we want to understand the values, morals, philosophies, aesthetics, and qualities of life in an historical period or geographic region (including our own), we study the arts of that time and place. If we want to contribute to the creation of our own culture in our own time, participation in the arts as creators, audience, or critics allows us an active role in the essential conversations of our communities and culture. Making art and actively appreciating the aesthetic dimensions of human creations are ways we transform our world from a random, chaotic place into a pleasing and even beautiful environment – a profound, but possible, transformation and one sorely needed in most of our schools.

Stevenson and Deasy have shown us schools in which this is exactly what has happened. Students have *moved* from passivity to activity, from being receivers to being creators. Teachers have done the same. Ironically, in most of our schools, being a teacher is often as passive as being a student. Teachers are conveyors of curriculum and assessment, not creators; they are discouraged from invention and improvisation and encouraged to stick to the 'program.' Indeed, programmed instruction is as prevalent in schools today as it has ever been. In this book, however, we see ten schools in which this transformation is underway. The arts provide the crucible for this alchemy.

The authors offer many answers to the question, "How does this transformation happen?" We have much to learn from their observations and the insights of those teachers, artists, administrators, and other researchers with whom they spoke. I am not surprised that the authors chose "third space" as their title for this book as that phrase points to what is perhaps the most essential element of this transformation – and also the most illusive. The idea of "third space" invites us to focus on that which might, at first glance, seem to be invisible. It is the "space between" teachers and learners, between the various individuals in a learning group, and between the learners, teachers, and works of art. This is the space in which meaning that has been negotiated and constructed by the members of a group emerges. When students, teachers and others (including administrators, parents, artists) gather around a work of art created by an artist or a student in the fourth grade and they strive to understand that work – what they see, what it means to each of them, what it makes them feel – they not only make sense of the work, they build community and understanding among themselves.

The beauty of the concept of "third space" is that it helps draw our attention to a space that is essential to learning and the creation of community – the place where connections are made. Arguably, making connections, along with identifying questions and having hypotheses, is a critical element of the process of building knowledge and understandings. Certainly, making connections is essential to the creation of effective and healthy communities. Negotiating differences in perspective, exploring alternative interpretations, and creating new solutions are all features of life in the "third spaces" of learning in and through the arts. They are also, I would argue, among the central processes of a true democracy.

Finally, it seems important to note one more feature of the arts that may explain their special role in the transformations described in this book. Among other qualities, the arts are attempts to understand both the common (experienced by most or all) and profound (of great seriousness and significance) aspects of what it means to be human. They explore experiences all of us are likely to have in our lifetimes – loss, love, fear, and moral confusions, for example. The arts strive to make visible and communicable that which eludes our general capacities to express, thus creating the possibility of forging connections between people on the ground of basic human experience.

I do not believe there is any other setting in schools that provides such an opportunity so well. Surely, the study of history, for example, can be a portal to this realm, but, as taught in most schools, it most often does not. This book suggests that the "third space" created through the study of the arts, when taught well, is a space in which students and teachers not only *can*, but *must*, be awake and in touch with one's humanity, including one's complex emotions and identities. It isn't hard to understand why children and young adults would prefer to spend their days in schools with many "third spaces" than those where these spaces rarely, if ever, exist. I certainly know which I would choose.

This book suggests an alternative vision of both the process and result of school reform. It points to reform that occurs not as a result of accountability measures, but as a natural transformation through the building of a new kind of community of learners, a community of creators. This book describes a "kinder, gentler" (to borrow from George Bush, Sr.) approach to school change, not based so much on punitive accountability, but rather on an invitation to create an exciting, meaningful, and more beautiful school. It is always good to have some alternatives in mind when trying to tackle as large a problem as the improvement of our public schools. This book provides such an alternative. I hope we can learn the lessons it offers.

Steve Seidel
Director, Project Zero
Director, Arts in Education Program,
Harvard Graduate School of Education

Preface

The Arts Education Partnership (AEP) was founded ten years ago during a surge of concern over the quality of public schools, a surge that led to the development of new federal and state laws, standards, and accountability systems. The concern first found a strong voice in the 1983 report, *A Nation at Risk,* that famously warned of a "rising tide of mediocrity" in American education.[1] The so-called "standards movement" prompted by the report gained momentum when the first President George Bush convened governors and corporate and educational leaders at a 1989 summit to set national goals for education. The federal *Goals 2000: Educate America Act*, passed in 1994 during the first administration of President Bill Clinton, incorporated these goals and demanded new actions by states to use the federal money provided by the law to improve their schools. The law named a set of subjects that should be taught to students in all schools. The arts were included.

The U.S. Secretary of Education at that time, Richard Riley, and Jane Alexander, then chair of the National Endowment for the Arts, were both strong arts education advocates, and believed the arts could play an important role in fulfilling the intention of the law. They jointly convened some 140 national education, arts, corporate, philanthropic, and civic organizations in a series of meetings to develop a coalition and plan for that purpose. In 1995 the two federal agencies entered into a cooperative agreement with the state departments of education through their national association, the Council of Chief State School Officers, and the state arts agencies through the National Assembly of State Arts Agencies to create an administrative entity that would support and convene the coalition and assist in implementing its plan. AEP was born and has since been sustained by continuous financing and guidance from these four agencies, carrying into the administration of the current President George Bush.

From the beginning, a fundamental concern of AEP has been to strengthen public understanding of the effects of learning and participation in the arts on the intellectual, personal, and social development of children and young people. Of equal concern has been the identification of schools, school districts, cultural organizations, and communities that engage students in quality arts activities. AEP has published a series of reports and research studies over the years to address these concerns. The reports are in wide use in schools, colleges, and communities throughout the country. *Third Space* is the latest and, in many respects, the most original and provocative of those publications. It both embraces and extends in important ways themes and findings from our previous research work.

Earlier Research

In 1998, AEP released one of its earliest reports on the impact of the arts, *Young Children and the Arts: Making Creative Connections*, showing the role of visual, auditory, and kinesthetic stimulation embodied in the arts in the cognitive and personal development of children from birth through grade three. In 1999 we published our study of public school districts throughout the country that sought to reach all students in their schools with arts instruction and participation. The study was done in cooperation with the President's Committee on the Arts and the Humanities and funded by the GE Fund (now GE Foundation). Ninety-one districts were featured in the report, *Gaining the Arts Advantage: Lessons from School Districts that Value Arts Education*. Factors identified in *Gaining* as important for implementing arts education in an entire district are now used in communities across the country to assess strengths and weaknesses in their arts policies and programs. A crucial finding was the essential role of communities external to the school in creating policy and political support for the arts and participating in partnerships with schools to provide quality arts programs for students.

A significant step forward in research on the effects of arts learning on students came with the 2000 publication of *Champions of Change: The Role of the Arts in Learning,* a set of seven studies supported by the GE Fund and the John D. and Catherine T. MacArthur Foundation, and published with their support by AEP, again in cooperation with the President's Committee on the Arts and the Humanities. Among the important findings in *Champions of Change* was the capacity of the arts to reach students who otherwise were not fully engaged by other school subjects and experiences.

The promising findings in *Champions of Change* prompted senior leaders at the U.S. Department of Education and the National Endowment for the Arts to fund AEP work in identifying and analyzing other research studies of the effects of arts education on young people's learning and to publish a compendium of the strongest of the studies. AEP released this compendium, *Critical Links: Learning in the Arts and Student Academic and Social Development,* in 2002. It was described by leadership of the American Educational Research Association as a benchmark for future arts education research. *Critical Links* analyzed and summarized findings from sixty-two studies of the effects of dance, drama, music, visual arts, and multi-arts experiences. The studies illuminate the profound and complex intellectual and emotional processes involved in learning the arts, and the interrelationships between those processes and student learning and development in other areas of school and life.

Among the significant implications of the *Critical Links* studies (reinforcing what we first reported in *Champions of Change*) was that while the arts had effects on all students, they could be particularly beneficial to students from economically disadvantaged circumstances and for students who typically had difficulty learning in school. These findings had enormous import for the challenges facing American education, specifically for strengthening the hand of schools with large populations of students from families of poverty. These so called "high poverty schools" often also include groups of students who are learning English for the first time, or who are assigned to special education classes, a percentage of whom are Black or Hispanic. These student groups tend to score lower on standardized tests and are the target of efforts to "close the achievement gap" as measured by these tests.

We saw indications in our studies that the arts helped these students to achieve, leading us to consider a study of schools with such populations at which students were succeeding and where the schools identified the arts as a reason for that success. In light of the positive effects of arts learning, we believed it was a matter of equity that schools extend the benefits of the arts to all students in the school, including those who struggle to learn. But, how might that be done?

Federal officials again expressed an interest in supporting our work. Congress provided funding through a grant from the U.S. Department of Education to develop and conduct the study. Likewise, generous support once again came from the GE Foundation. The Ford Foundation added its support while the project was in progress. Lauren Stevenson, senior associate for research on the AEP staff, and the assistant editor of *Critical Links,* led the study. *Third Space* tells the story of what she and her team of researchers found.

That story has wider implications than we initially believed for the daunting problems facing American students and schools. While the arts can indeed engage students in ways that contribute to their success on standard measures of achievement, we began to see that they play an even richer and more profound role in preparing students to cope in the present and contribute in the future in an America and a world of enormous opportunities and equally enormous conflicts. As one of the educators interviewed for the study put it, the arts give students a centered life from which to navigate through their present and their future.

The challenge to American education has never been simply to raise test scores — that is a relatively recent and limited goal. The challenge has always been to raise citizens who are capable of active participation in the social, cultural, political, and economic life of the world's longest experiment in democracy, an experiment demanding a free, educated, and committed citizenry. We were amazed to discover anew the role of the arts in realizing that vision and creating that democracy. That is the larger story we believe *Third Space* can tell. That is why we offer it as a compelling reason to fully embrace the arts in our schools. It's how to sustain our democracy.

Richard J. Deasy
Director
Arts Education Partnership

Introduction

This started out as a very different kind of book. The research project described in these pages originally set out to examine arts instruction in ten case study schools with the goal of identifying strategies that educators could use to improve schools serving economically disadvantaged communities. We thought we would share the lessons learned from the case studies in a how-to manual for school leaders. What we found at the schools we studied surprised us, however, and demanded an altogether different kind of book.

The lessons from the schools were not only a matter of strategies, programs, and procedures, but a more complex, nuanced, and profound story about how the arts change schools. We found that the arts connected schools with their communities and enabled them to create powerful contexts and conditions for learning–contexts and conditions which we came to call *third space*. It is this latter story that we tell in this book.

The Research Question

In spring 2001 the Arts Education Partnership (AEP) posed the question, "How do the arts contribute to the improvement of schools that serve economically disadvantaged communities?" In summer 2001 Dick Deasy invited me to join the AEP staff to design a research project to explore this question, beginning what was to become a four-year journey.

As is typical of work at AEP, the project unfolded as a series of collaborations. AEP is a coalition of over a hundred arts and education organizations nationwide, connecting researchers, practitioners, and policy makers at the forefront of arts and education. When AEP designs its projects, it draws upon the expertise of these groups in designing work of a high standard that will be useful and relevant to those working in the field.

A Wide Lens

Our first step was to design a framework for the research. We did so with the advice of a group of researchers who had recently completed a compendium with AEP that analyzed and synthesized research studies examining links between learning in the arts and student academic and social development. This compendium, *Critical Links*, and the work of the individual researchers illuminated the types of outcomes that we might expect to see associated with arts learning. We carefully considered the ramifications that this set of outcomes could have for our case study schools.

We deliberately chose a wide lens through which to look at the connections between the arts programs in the schools and school quality. Judgments about school quality frequently rest primarily on the scores of students on standardized tests in reading and mathematics – an important but limited measure. We were interested in taking a wider and deeper look, incorporating standardized test scores into a more comprehensive picture of a school's success.

Our research advisors provided guidance as we developed a diverse set of indicators of school quality that included students' academic, personal, and social development; teacher efficacy, satisfaction, and professional growth; school culture and climate; and community involvement. These indicators became the basis for the questions that guided our interviews and observations when we conducted our field research.

The Case Study Schools

AEP's partner organizations nominated possible case study sites – schools with outstanding arts programs, in which at least fifty percent of the students were from economically disadvantaged families. When possible, we sought schools that had been the subject of other research or evaluation studies that provided evidence of the quality of their arts programs, or that had been singled out as highly successful by national or state recognition programs. Our goal was not to demonstrate that the schools deserved their reputations but rather to explore how and why the schools believed that their arts programs were crucial to their success, and what strategies had been essential to the implementation of the programs.

We developed a list of schools that met the criteria we had established, looking closely for overlap in the recommendations. We conducted phone interviews with school district personnel where the most promising sites were located and with the principals, staff, and community partners of the individual schools. Based on these conversations, we selected a set of ten schools for further consideration. The schools included were elementary, middle, and high schools in geographically diverse urban and rural communities.

Representatives from each of the ten schools were invited to participate in a two-day forum in Phoenix, Arizona, in January 2002, to discuss how the arts can contribute to whole school reform, improving and sustaining a school's overall quality and performance. The forum was one of three that AEP conducts annually to engage researchers and practitioners in addressing critical issues in arts and education. The schools presented and discussed their arts programs in small group sessions with AEP staff and other meeting participants. The forum thus served as an additional means of vetting the potential of the invited schools to function as case studies for the research project. Eight of the ten schools were subsequently included in the project.

In spring 2002, we began site visits to the schools. A small team of researchers with experience in arts education research joined AEP in conducting the field work. Two researchers, myself and another member of the team, visited each of the schools. In the course of these two-day visits, we interviewed teachers, students, artists, administrators, families, and representatives of community arts and education organizations working with the schools. We recorded all interviews for transcription and analysis.

An Added Focus

By summer 2002 we had completed visits to four of the case study schools. Though our findings were tentative at that stage, AEP's director Dick Deasy and I began sharing them with colleagues and discussing them at conferences and meetings, including a Ford Foundation seminar on its new initiative to support arts education in urban areas. We shared with Ford early indications that the arts were improving the relationships between students, teachers, and other community members at the schools. The arts, it seemed, helped to build understanding among diverse groups of students as well as a sense of school community.

Ford was interested in the question of how the arts could foster a commitment to pluralism and a shared sense of community in schools, a crucial challenge they recognized for the country as a whole. Ford offered support to focus in our project on the community-building potential of the arts. The decision to do so had significant consequences for the entire study and for the findings reported in *Third Space.*

With Ford's support, we convened a small team of researchers to develop an additional set of questions that would allow us to take a closer look at the nature of community in the remaining site visit schools; to see whether the arts were playing a role in shaping that community; and if so, to determine what could be learned from the process that could benefit other schools. The community lens allowed us to look more closely at the relationships in the schools and how these relationships changed in the presence of the arts.

A third researcher joined us on each of the remaining site visits to conduct the necessary additional interviews using this new set of questions. At that time, we added two additional case study schools to the study, responding to the need to include another high school and another middle school. This brought the total to ten. The final six school site visits were completed in fall 2002.

The Analysis and Interpretation of Data

Following each site visit, researchers completed initial reports for the schools that they visited. Combing these reports and our interview transcripts, I produced a first draft of the themes that were emerging from the data, and in March 2003, we convened the majority of the researchers who had participated in the site visits to reflect upon, interrogate, and extend these themes. We continued our analysis with the guidance they provided.

In the fall, we held a similar meeting with representatives from each of the case study schools. As we had with the researchers, we shared the central themes drawn out in our analysis—by then more defined—for their reflection and comment. The schools concurred with our analysis and told us they thought that we had captured well the central tenets of their work. Over a day and a half meeting, we held discussions to refine the emerging framework for reporting the findings of the study.

Two Perspectives Emerge

It became clear in the later stages of our analysis of the data that we had two major stories to tell. One had to do with the processes and procedures through which the schools built and sustained their arts education programming, making it a part of the fabric of the school. Included in this story were factors that the schools saw as important to their success, and practical lessons they had to share with other schools. This was essentially the story that we had set out to tell.

The second story had to do with the nature and effects of the arts programming—the ways in which it seemed to be changing what school was about, and the new opportunities it created for teaching and learning and for building community within and around the schools. The first story was about *how* and the latter about *what* and *why*. We faced an important decision about which of these stories we would tell in this book.

A team of school leaders—two principals, one state education official, and one teacher educator—gave us important guidance. We had asked for their assistance in the early stages of the project because they were representative of the audience we thought the project would have—school leaders. They counseled us then on how to present our findings most usefully to that audience. Together, we had imagined an easy-to-use manual, complete with tabs and tables. When we sought their advice at this later stage of the project, however, they pointed us in a new direction.

They had reviewed a draft of the book and were struck by the discussions of the changes that occurred in the schools for students, teachers, and families. They believed that this set of stories had profound implications for the way we in the United States think about and define the purposes of school. They urged us to make this the focus of the book and to widen our audience to those more generally concerned about public education.

At this meeting we discussed with them the metaphor of *third space* encountered in one of our school visits, a metaphor which we felt could be the framework for the discussion of the changes we saw happening at the schools. Despite the initial ambiguity the term held for them, they recommended that we embrace the metaphor in the title of the book and in the interpretation of our findings. They believed the term could be a signal to readers that new thinking about teaching and learning was essential, and that the arts had an important role to play in changing education. "Tell that story," the administrators advised. That is what we have tried to do.

The Book

In developing the final text of *Third Space,* Dick Deasy and I shared successive drafts with researchers and with staff at the case study schools. Their thoughtful comments helped us to refine the telling of the schools' stories.

In Chapter 1, we set the stage for these stories, defining third space and introducing the schools and their arts education programs. We look in Chapter 2 at the importance of third space for students, elaborating upon how the arts help learning to become meaningful and relevant to them, and how the arts help students to develop a strong sense of self. In Chapter 3 we explore the kinds of thinking skills and capacities students develop in the arts. In Chapter 4 we look at the ramifications of arts learning for language and literacy development. In Chapter 5 we discuss the changes in schools from the perspectives of teachers — how the arts increase their satisfaction and efficacy in teaching. Finally, in Chapter 6, we explore how the arts build a sense of community within and around the schools.

We share the stories of what is occurring in the schools through the voices and artwork of their students, teachers, artists, families, and administrators. We do our best to honor their work and to convey its importance to the national debate about the purpose and design of the public school.

Lauren M. Stevenson
Senior Associate for Research
Arts Education Partnership

Beginnings

Take a look around you
There are opposites everywhere
Three sections to this book
 We've given our fair share
Animals, people, nature too
Many things to reflect by you
Everything has it's own perspective
Everyone's view must be respected
Every poem within this book
Contains a shelf of special looks
Even though you may not agree
Keep your mind open and free

fig. 1 Beginnings, poem by Madeline; collage by Andrew, Peter Howell Elementary School

1

Third Space: Creating the Conditions for Learning

"You feel like you're doing something amazing and incredible."

— STUDENT, CENTRAL FALLS HIGH SCHOOL, CENTRAL FALLS, RHODE ISLAND

Fourth-grade students at Peter Howell Elementary School in Tucson, Arizona, created a book of poetry on the theme of opposites. Working with their classroom teacher, principal, and a visual artist, they wrote and illustrated their poems, including a set juxtaposing "beginnings" and "endings." Though the moments are opposites in some ways – openings versus closings of experiences – the students express in these poems that beginnings and endings share something in common. They are both enhanced by an open mind and a willingness to see new possibilities. In a beginning, an open mind allows you to be available to learning and to seeing things in a new and often unexpected way. An ending can invite you to imagine the world anew based on the experience that has just come to a close – to experiment with what that experience might allow you to see and do that you couldn't before. We propose these two poems, *Beginnings* and *Endings*, as bookends, invitations to be open to the possibilities that the arts offer for re-creating schools (see figure 1).

This openness was important for us in coming to understand the work of the schools we studied and describe in this book. The impact of their arts programming was more complex and far reaching than we had expected. A large body of research on the effects of the arts in schools has looked at what is called *transfer*—how a particular intellectual or social skill developed by participation in the arts prepares students for learning and success in another area of school or life. The changes that we saw in the schools were more fundamental and more powerful than these one-to-one transfer associations. By forging new relationships between artists, students, and teachers, the arts created powerful contexts and conditions for learning in which students played active and meaningful roles in their own education and through which a sense of community was formed within and around the schools. We began to see that the lessons offered by these schools address not only public concerns about how well students learn but how schools can promote the principles and practices of a democratic society.

Third Space

We borrow the term *third space* from a teaching artist at the Sheridan Global Arts and Communications School in Minneapolis, Minnesota. Third space describes the sets of relationships forged by the arts and the context these relationships create for teaching and learning. The artist used the term to capture the atmosphere in the classroom when she and her students create works of art, one in which students are deeply absorbed and able to take the risks demanded in a creative process.

The term third space has a history in the arts in describing the way in which meaning exists, not in a viewer alone (the first space) or a piece of art (the second space), but in the interaction between the two—where the viewer brings his or her own experiences and imagination to bear in the interpretation of the artwork.[2]

A similar third space is opened in the process of *creating* a work of art. The space is one between the artist and his or her medium in which the artist's imagination and skill combine with formal elements of an art form to create an artifact rich in meaning that stands on its own. This space allows the artist to try out and explore new ideas. In collaborative art forms, members of an ensemble enter this space together to create their work of art. They take on new identities, such as characters in theater, as they explore relationships and meanings with others in the space.

We liked the term third space because it packed into a single metaphor the changes that students, teachers, artists, parents, and principals said happened to them and to their schools when the arts were made a central feature of a school's philosophy and programs. The term captured the rich environment that the arts created for learning, not just for learning the arts themselves but for learning other disciplines such as mathematics, social studies, language arts, history, and science and for linking that learning to the concerns and daily lives of students.

The Arts

The arts are present in a variety of ways in the ten schools. The profiles of the individual schools at the end of the book describe the details of their specific programs. The arts instruction at all of the schools includes both a selection of discrete arts classes – classes in visual art, music, dance, or theater – and integrated arts instruction. In integrated arts lessons, arts and non-arts content and skills are taught in tandem, with the content and methods of the disciplines woven together for mutual reinforcement.

Discrete arts classes are typically taught by teachers trained in an art form in undergraduate and postgraduate programs and licensed by their state to teach the arts. We refer to these teachers as *arts specialists*. Integrated arts programs carry the challenge of helping teachers of non-arts subjects develop a level of understanding and competence in an art form that will enable them to teach it effectively in their classes, and to make what the national associations of arts teachers call "authentic connections" between the art form and the other subjects they teach.[3] At the schools, these teachers were sometimes trained to deliver integrated instruction by themselves, but more frequently, they worked with an artist in their classrooms to develop and deliver integrated instruction. These artists were sometimes the school's arts specialists and sometimes artists from the local community, called *teaching artists*.[4] Both teaching artists and arts specialists brought passion and expertise in their art form to the school and became models – living standards, if you will – of what students and teachers were striving to learn.

Under the best circumstances the partnerships between teachers and artists from the community consist of active collaborations in which they work together to help each other and their students find the authentic connections between their disciplines. This collaboration deepens when the teaching artist spends an extended period working with school staff in what is referred to as an *artist residency*. Every school we visited drew on arts, cultural, and higher education organizations in their communities to varying degrees in order to form these collaborations.

The arts saturate each of the schools. Visual art is displayed on walls; music is played in the halls; exhibitions and performances are presented in classes, auditoriums, and community settings. In some cases daytime arts programs spill over into activities before and after school. Parents get involved as audience members and teachers, some even joining their children for arts lessons at the school. Community arts organizations perform in the schools; students attend exhibitions and performances at galleries, museums, and concert halls.

The Schools

The schools described in this book represent many of the complex conditions found in public education systems across America. The schools are urban and rural. They have large numbers of students learning English as a second language and receiving special education services. All of them serve student populations that statistically can be called "high poverty"; at least half the students in each school are from families with incomes below the poverty line, with numbers much higher in most of the schools. Schools like these often battle poor public images and low expectations for success. The commitment that the schools we studied made to the arts enabled them to show the fallacy of these low expectations, make visible their true potential, and succeed for their students.

Included among the ten schools are four elementary schools: Newton D. Baker School of Arts in Cleveland, Ohio; Peter Howell Elementary School in Tucson, Arizona; Pierce Street Elementary School in Tupelo, Mississippi; and P.S. 130 in Brooklyn, New York. Two of the ten schools serve kindergarten through eighth-grade students: Grizzly Hill on the San Juan Ridge in California; and Sheridan Global Arts and Communications School in Minneapolis, Minnesota. Two are middle schools: Hand Middle School in Columbia, South Carolina; and Clarkton School of Discovery in Clarkton, North Carolina. Two are high schools: Central Falls High School in Central Falls, Rhode Island; and Dyett Academic Center High School in Chicago, Illinois.[5]

The scope of the arts' influence varied in the ten schools. In general, schools with elementary and middle school students had more success in establishing a school-wide commitment to the arts. In contrast, relatively small but vibrant arts-centered communities existed at the two high schools, where the departmental organization typical of high schools appeared to challenge the ability to make a school-wide impact. In each of these high schools the arts programming began not at the administrative level but at the grass roots through the influence of highly committed artists and teachers. At both schools the arts programs were beginning to expand their reach. This was particularly true at Central Falls High School, where the programs had a longer history. As a teacher there said, arts programs are beginning to "creep" into new classrooms as more teachers see their value.

School Change

Changing a school is not an easy task. A school needs a vision for what it wants to be—an image of excellence to express its values, arouse its energies, guide its actions, shape its programs, portray itself to itself and to its communities. The power of a vision to transform a school lies in whether it truly engages those in the school and in the community in ways they find meaningful and rewarding. Ultimately, the vision must grow out of and perpetuate a sense of shared purpose and community. This vision must inspire and support teaching and learning

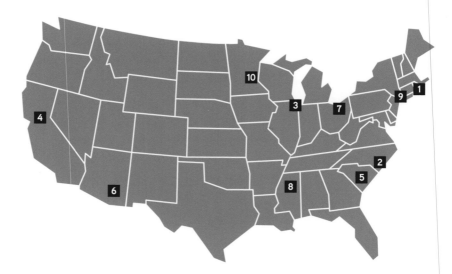

1 **Central Falls High School**
Grades 9-12
Central Falls, RI

2 **Clarkton School of Discovery**
Grades 6-8
Clarkton, NC

3 **Dyett Academic Center High School**
Grades 7-12
Chicago, IL

4 **Grizzly Hill School**
Grades K-8
San Juan Ridge, CA

5 **Hand Middle School**
Grades 6-8
Columbia, SC

6 **Peter Howell Elementary School**
Grades K-5
Tucson, AZ

7 **Newton D. Baker School of Arts**
Grades K-5
Cleveland, OH

8 **Pierce Street Elementary**
Grades K-3
Tupelo, MS

9 **P.S. 130**
Grades PK-5
Brooklyn, NY

10 **Sheridan Global Arts
and Communications School**
Grades K-8
Minneapolis, MN

that matters to students and teachers, otherwise it will simply generate a new set of rules and regulations to be enforced rather than embraced. It will become a set of procedures put and held in place by rewards and sanctions designed by authorities. Mastery of procedures will be valued more highly than creativity and innovation; success measured by test results more than by multiple demonstrations of deep understanding and personal development; and organizational conformity fostered more than community. In whole or in part, the schools we studied were seeking these richer forms of change and achievement and they found the possibility for it in the arts.

Each of the schools revealed to us that its success related to the seriousness with which students, teachers, and administrators embraced the arts as profound explorations and expressions of self, others, and the world – explorations and expressions that were deeply meaningful to students. The arts, when they were seen and taught with this understanding, were capable of generating new sets of relationships – third spaces – among all those in the school and the community. ■

2

When Learning Matters

"[S]chools must make students believe and feel that they are respected and that they belong, that they can learn what they are required to learn, and that the lessons of school 'make sense' within the context of their own lives."

— DEBORAH STIPEK, ET AL., *ENGAGING SCHOOLS: FOSTERING HIGH SCHOOL STUDENTS' MOTIVATION TO LEARN*[6]

The arts help to make learning matter to students. In the schools we studied, the arts put students in active and meaningful roles in their classrooms and connected schools to student's lives and cultures. They opened possibilities for students to contribute to their communities and made learning an authentic project in which students explored not only the content of academic subjects but their own lives and identities.

In using the term "matter" to describe these qualities that the arts bring to learning, we build on a seminal National Research Council report on positive youth development.[7] Researchers write in the report that because young people must necessarily be "agents of their own development" settings that support positive youth development "need to be youth centered, providing youth—both individually and in groups—the opportunity to be efficacious and to make a difference in their social worlds," an opportunity they call "mattering."[8]

"Mattering" was the central concept that teachers, students, and school administrators expressed when they described the impact the arts had on student learning, and why arts learning experiences engaged students in different and more powerful ways than other school programs. Learning mattered to students, they said, and students felt like they mattered in their schools.

In the third space created by the arts – in classrooms, before and after school programs, and community activities where the arts were present – teaching and learning was student-centered, and students became agents of their own learning. "With the arts in the classroom, I was more involved. We got to bring our own ideas," a student at Central Falls High School in Rhode Island put it succinctly. Students were empowered to learn and to be efficacious in their social worlds within and beyond school.

Student as Artist

The demands of the role of artist are different than the demands typically placed on students in schools. A work of art is expected to be original and expressive, a personal statement in an art form and not just a work that shows a teacher a student's skill with the form's materials and processes. Art is fundamentally a work of its maker. Student artists are expected to bring to their work not only an understanding of the artistic form but something that is uniquely theirs, something of what Maxine Greene refers to as a "lived world."[9] In the arts, a third space is opened where students draw on their "lived world" (a first space) and what they have learned from their teachers (a second space) to create and express something new, something no one else could have made. Art by its nature requires and demands this of them. This demand sets teaching and learning in the arts apart from that in many other school subjects, in which students are limited to working with the materials and knowledge they acquire in class – where they are expected to return virtually identical responses to a given assignment (see figure 2).

These dynamics of the arts learning experience are visible, for example, in the senior projects done by visual art students in the Human Creativity art program at Central Falls High School in Rhode Island, a program consisting of a cluster of school day and after school visual and performing arts classes. The students work over the course of their last semester at the school on a project of their own choosing, a single artwork which will be exhibited for the school at the end of the year. As part of the assignment, students are asked to conduct in-depth research on a particular art technique, artist, or both. The research is the starting point for the assignment. Students have to use it as a source of inspiration as they create an original work.

One student, for example, chose to make a quilt because it was a traditional art form of the women in her family. She studied the life and work of Faith Ringgold, the American artist famous for her paint-ed quilts and the stories they tell. The student then created a quilt of her own, its shapes and colors symbolic of different facets of her fam-ily history. Four inlaid paintings on the quilt each tell the story of a particular female relative (see figure 3). The work was an amalgam of what she had learned in her research – quilt-making techniques and the life and artistic accomplishments of Ringgold – and her knowledge and understanding of her own family.

When students participate in this kind of arts learning experience, their imaginations and personal backgrounds are part of the content of their work, part of the meaning that they are making. As a teaching artist at Dyett Academic Center High School in Chicago said, the arts "allow students to pull their life experiences into the text of school and public life." They allow students to be valued in schools in new ways and for learning to be more relevant to them.

Exploring Possible Selves

An important way that learning in the arts mattered to students was the opportunity that it offered to explore their own identities and to express themselves. The arts are acts of the imagination, what Maxine Greene calls the ability to envision things "as if they might be other-wise."[10] They are a medium in which students can imagine and try out new possibilities for themselves and their futures.

"Art tells me something about myself." "Art is something you can tell to your friends through your work's expression." "You express the

fig. 2

Art is Life
By Ashley, Grizzly Hill School

To me, Art is Life. Most people look at life from the outside. They see what appears to be there, on the surface. For instance, someone might look at an apple and just see something delicious to eat. When I look at an apple I see something amazing. People say that magic doesn't exist. What they don't know is that magic is all around them. That apple is full of life. It's beautiful!

When Henry David Thoreau said, "The perception of beauty is a moral test," he meant that anyone can see things as they appear to be, but that the test of life is to see the real beauty that lies beneath the surface of everything. An artist has the ability to look around and realize that nothing is as it appears to be on the surface. An artist looks deep and sees the Life in everything. During the darkest, saddest times or the brightest, happiest times, the artist helps others to look within themselves and beneath the surface of everything.

I've studied and studied this and I still don't fully understand it. It's a mystery to me, something that can't really be explained, even though I experience it. Everything can be viewed as Art. I see every detail of an object and am fascinated by its existence. Most people see the world around them filled with things that are used and then forgotten. Artists keep those things alive. Even if the subject comes from the artists' imaginations, those artists continue to live through their art.

I really liked the way the cavemen expressed themselves. They drew pictures of life the way it was then. It's almost as if they were keeping themselves and their world alive through their art. We can look at one of those cave paintings and tell what life was like for them. We can see what kind of animals were there.

It's all a part of the Great Mystery of Life. Albert Einstein said, "The most beautiful thing we can experience is the Mysterious. It is the source of all true art and science." I feel as though he understood how I feel. Art has influenced me by making me want to discover the Mystery of Life.

fig. 3 Destiny, mixed media by Anyeli, Central Falls High School

emotions of your soul when you paint." "Art is everyday life. It shows your true colors," is how elementary students at Newton D. Baker School of Arts in Cleveland answered the question "What is Art?" on a poster that hung in the school hallway.

The arts also provide students a safe space in which to conduct self-exploration. An art form – a play, a mural, a recital – is a third space, a mediating zone of safety in which students can take risks. Students may try out new identities in works of art to which others can respond, experimenting with possibilities within the safety of the art form.

A fifth-grade teacher at P.S. 130 in Brooklyn was explicit about the way in which theater, for example, created the possibilities for the risk-taking necessary for self-exploration: "You have to know your lines, you have to be the person you're portraying, which is good for the students because some of the shy ones are now not themselves, but the characters they're playing and so they find it easier to express themselves." A fifth-grade student at P.S. 130 similarly said that the theater artist working in his classroom "always tells us when we go up in front of the class, we're not ourselves, we're a different person, and I just feel comfortable that way." As characters, students are safe to explore relationships, ideas, meanings, and possible selves.

The third space opened in the arts is a space to both lose and find yourself. In all of the schools, arts learning experiences built on this

fig. 4 What's My Story?, mixed media by Fa, Sheridan Global Arts and Communications School

fig. 5 *What's My Story?*, photograph by Samantha,
Sheridan Global Arts and Communications School

potential. Many made self-exploration and self-identity an explicit
focus. At Sheridan Global Arts and Communications School in
Minneapolis, Minnesota, for example, students worked with their
teachers and bookmaking artists on a project called *What's My Story?*
In this project, students used photography to document aspects of
their family and community lives that were important to them. They
then wrote stories about the images and compiled them into hand-
made *What's My Story?* books (see figures 4 and 5).

At Clarkton School of Discovery in rural North Carolina, visual art students created portraits of themselves as they would look in ten years—a young woman in the seventh grade depicted herself as a blooming flower (see figure 6); a young man showed himself as an older artist (see figure 7).

fig. 6 The Future, print by Tiffany, Clarkton School of Discovery

WHEN LEARNING MATTERS

fig. 7 Ten Years from Now, drawing by Ari, Clarkton School of Discovery

Their art teacher said the assignment reflects her belief that, "Art is a place where you express who you are." She said that the young man's portrait of his future self—an image she sees as strong, confident, and serious—presents an interesting contrast to one he had done of how he currently sees himself, a portrait he had called *The Player*. The young woman's self-portrait employed the metaphor of an opening flower to directly connect her present self of innate potential to a more fully realized future self.

In a similar assignment at Central Falls High School, Human Creativity students created self-portraits that communicated, as their teacher put it, "who they were beyond, 'this is what I look like.'" The portraits were to be more than just a physical representation of themselves. Students fulfilled the assignment in different ways; some made literal physical depictions of themselves expressing their character and emotion through posture and facial expression (see figure 8). Others conveyed their identities in abstract compositions (see figure 9). Like the students at the Clarkton School of Discovery, they imagined and depicted identities and futures in an exploratory way.

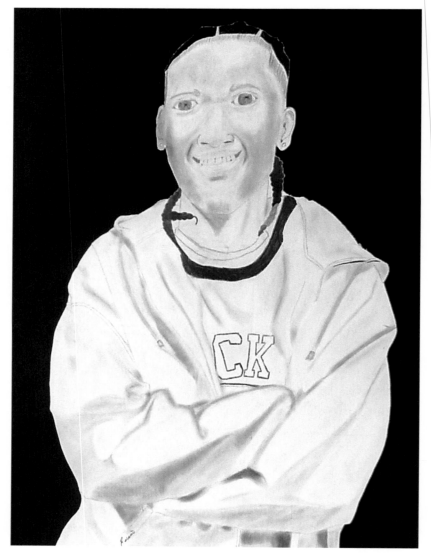

fig. 8 Self-portrait, drawing by Ambiori, Central Falls High School

fig. 9 I'm Lost, drawing by Jasmine, Central Falls High School

A former student of Central Falls High School said about her experience in Human Creativity, "I really love this school because I've seen my future in this school and I'm proud of myself." "I learned how to express myself and open my mind in front of people – my feelings, my dreams, my decisions," another student said. "My imagination was so closed until Human Creativity. When I came here I started to express myself, to show people who I really was, what I really feel, who I'm really going to be some day." Another said, "The arts open up kids and allow them to express the emotions they feel at home like other subjects can't."

An artist teaching at Sheridan Global Arts and Communications School said similarly, "I think we are giving kids another way to express themselves besides being mad or angry. There is a deeper, personal, individual thing happening when they learn there is another way to express themselves." As a student at Central Falls puts it, "You get something off your chest" (see figure 10).

As a result of the arts programming at P.S. 130, the school's new assistant principal said the students there are different from students at other schools where she's worked. P.S. 130 students "have a center"– they are grounded.

Student comments and artwork at the schools reflected a statement made by philosopher of arts and education, Elliot Eisner, in *Arts and*

fig. 10

Bad Memories
By John, Grizzly Hill School

Memories of the bad things I remember
Sometimes they come back

I try to hide them but they come back
I try to bury them but they don't stay

I try to burn them but they're not flammable
I try to throw them away but they boomerang back

I try to get rid of them but can't
Maybe just maybe they'll go away when I'm 6 feet deep
in thought

the Creation of Mind: "Work in the arts is not only a way of creating performances and products; it is a way of creating our lives."[11] "The arts, if they are about anything, are about the creation of a personal vision."[12]

The Impact of Contributing

The arts are meant to be performed or exhibited. They culminate in a real product that has meaning to students, a product they can share with others – a teacher, classmates, the whole school, parents, the community. The prospect of exhibiting or performing their artwork endows the arts learning experience with a purpose that focuses energies and heightens the importance of its challenges, adding another dimension to the power of the arts to matter to students.

Students learn "how to make a real thing that has value to society; it helps them feel good about themselves," said a teacher at Sheridan Global Arts and Communications School about the books that students create working with their classroom teachers and local bookmaking artists, as in the *What's My Story?* project. The students learn how to hand make paper and book covers; how to bind into books their own visual art and writing, often poetry (see figure 11). When their books are complete, students do readings of their work in a local coffee shop and bookstore. They have real audiences for their work.

Across the ten schools, this dimension of the arts learning experience—that it culminates in a product that has value to oneself and to an external audience—engaged students in school and allowed them to feel as though what they were doing and learning in school was impor-

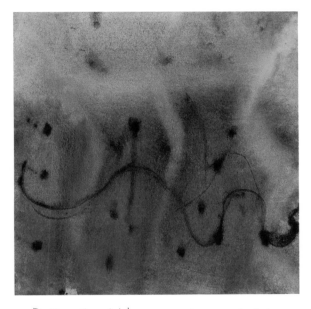

Bright yellow lightning scares the gray clouds! The cold fast wind was so cold it made the scariness go away. The clouds thanked the wind. "Thankyou thankyou. wind, your so generous," the clouds said. "Generous. He is just the wind, why would he be generous?" said the Lightning laughing loud.

fig. 11 Watercolor and text from the book *Painting the Sky* by Krista, Sheridan Global Arts and Communications School tant. In their 1999 report for the National Research Council, *How People Learn: Brain, Mind, Experience, and School*, cognitive scientist John Bransford and his colleagues explain that learning experiences that culminate in products of this kind can be particularly motivating for students. "Feeling that one is contributing something to others," they write, "appears to be especially motivating. For example, young learners are highly motivated to write stories and draw pictures that they can share with others... Learners of all ages are more motivated when they can see the usefulness of what they are learning and when they can use that information to do something that has an impact on others — especially their local community."[13]

At Newton D. Baker School of Arts, the faculty has institutionalized a practice that epitomizes their understanding of the importance of allowing students to contribute to others. The school enrolls students in kindergarten through grade five.[14] Each year the graduating fifth graders design and paint a mural in a school hallway as their legacy to the school. The curriculum across all grades at Newton D. Baker is designed around an annual theme and the fifth graders are asked to create a mural to honor this theme and the work that students and teachers have done together throughout the year. Often the students also pay tribute to a particular artist that they've studied in conjunction with the school-wide theme by attempting to paint in the artist's style. The year we visited Newton D. Baker, the school-wide theme was Native American history and culture and the fifth-grade students painted a mural on the school lockers paying tribute to the painting of Native American artist Helen Hardin (see figure 12).

Educational researcher Bonnie Benard expresses the value of these activities this way: "When opportunities for participation incorporate opportunities for contribution, and youth are able to 'give back' their gifts to their families, schools, and communities, they no longer see themselves as simply recipients of what adults have to offer... but as active contributors to the settings in which they live. Giving back is a powerful 'hook' for all youth, especially for those not used to thinking of themselves as successful."[15]

fig. 12 Mural by fifth-grade students, Newton D. Baker School of Arts

A teaching artist at Sheridan Global Arts and Communications School said similarly, "Parents like [the arts in the school] because they're able to see their students really being successful in something tangible – projects, a card, a book, something that they've made. For kids who haven't had a lot of success in school, that's huge for them."

This opportunity to be successful in school is particularly important for many of Sheridan's students who have recently immigrated to the United States and do not yet read or speak English. Without the opportunity to participate in the arts, many of these students may face a long wait until they are able to accomplish something that is visible and recognized – through typical school measures – as meaningful or successful.

The awareness across the ten schools of the importance of creating opportunities for students to give something of themselves back to the school community paralleled the findings of educational and policy researcher Milbrey McLaughlin in her ten-year study of community-based programs that made a difference in the lives of young people. "[T]he youth organizations that attracted and sustained young people's involvement," the study found, "gave visible and ongoing voice to a conception of youth as a resource to be developed and as persons of value to themselves and to society.... Youth activities geared toward tangible products or performances provide a sense of accomplishment and success."[16] For many students in the case study schools, the arts are the most tangible products and performances through which they establish their presence to the school and society.

Self-Efficacy

Learning in the arts helps students to develop a sense of self-efficacy, a feeling that they can be agents of their own learning and that they can make positive change in their own lives and in their surroundings.

A parent at the Sheridan Global Arts and Communications School described this quality of the arts learning experience: "At least for my three children, the performance aspect of presenting their work is about self-esteem and the development of that self-esteem comes out in all of the areas, comes through in the classroom, regardless of whether the area of study is beyond the arts. The ability to stand up and express an idea and back up that idea with feelings and to be themselves.... I think all three of my children have established a personality that comes out and they're not afraid to express themselves. And I think that's a tribute to the Sheridan education."

The drama teacher at Hand Middle School in Columbia, South Carolina, expressed in an interesting way her view of the relationship between the arts and a student's growing sense of self-esteem. She said, "I don't think the arts teach self-esteem and confidence; I think the arts *demand* self-esteem and confidence." Because an artist is making a uniquely personal work and will expose it to public view, the process calls for a sense of self that can navigate the anxieties and risks of possible rejection or failure.

As students grow in competence and assurance in expressing themselves in an art form — a painting, a poem, a dance — they not only grow more assured and confident but also have a sense of accomplishment and a growing understanding that they can make an even greater

fig. 13 Students at Hand Middle School prepare costumes for a performance.

impact as their work becomes more skillful (see figure 13). They want to get better, to learn more. In this way, they grow not just in self-esteem – a feeling good about one's self – but in *self-efficacy*, the belief that one's actions can make a difference (see figure 14). Benard calls these "mastery experiences" and says "having mastery experiences is one of the most effective means of developing a sense of efficacy." "Perceived self-efficacy," she adds, "plays a major role in educational success in terms of both motivation and achievement."[17]

Engagement

As the arts create a space for learning that is student-centered and mean-ingfully connected to students' lives – where learning matters – students, teachers, and parents at the schools said they noticed students' disposi-tions toward school changing. Students, they said, became more engaged in school. "If it wasn't for this program, I wouldn't be in school at this point," a student in the Human Creativity arts program at Central Falls High School said straightforwardly.

fig. 14

Transformations
By Maria, Grizzly Hill School

Before I came here
I was a bird gliding on the cool breeze
    a tree growing towards the sky
    a blade of grass in a field
a strand of silk holding together a scarf.

Now I am here.
I am a horse grazing in a pasture
    a shadow of a girl running
        through a field of flowers
    the water in the stream
    a star in the evening sky.

Soon I shall
Be a golden feather in a bird's wing
    a petal on a rose
    a flower in a garden
    a dolphin in the sea.

The arts coordinator at Pierce Street Elementary school said, "Our kids cry at the end of school because they don't want to go home; this is such a happy place for them." "Art makes learning more meaningful to the students," she added. "They are very proud. People walk in here from other schools and they're so impressed with what's on the walls" (see figure 15).

A group of parents at Peter Howell Elementary School in Tucson, Arizona, talked about the new enthusiasm for school and for learning they saw in their children since the school adopted an arts focus, a program of the Tucson Unified School District called Opening Minds Through the Arts. They described changes in attitude and behavior by their children at school and at home.

"My kids are always talking about things they are doing at school," a mother said. "They didn't use to be like this. Now they want to tell us about all the classes they are taking and the trips they are going to go on. My son comes home just incredibly excited about the whole thing and tells me everything, and he is very detailed."

fig. 15 Students admire artwork at Pierce Street Elementary School.

"They read more and read more different things" another parent said. "They don't want to miss school because they will miss something. They are getting better grades, but even better, they like school."

The level of engagement among Human Creativity art students at Central Falls High School, coupled with their fear that the program might be eliminated in response to the chronically fragile finances of the school, led them to form a research team to track the attendance, discipline referral rates, grade point averages, and college applications and acceptances for students in the program. They found that Human Creativity students compare favorably to other Central Falls students on these measures.

Parents, teachers, and administrators at other schools also attributed good or improving student behavior and attendance rates to their arts programs. The interim superintendent for Pierce Street Elementary School's district said, for example, "Attendance is excellent at Pierce Street," and discipline referrals are "among the lowest in the district for those grades." He and school faculty members credited the school's arts integrated curriculum for these statistics.

Because a variety of school, home, and community conditions affect school attendance, it is difficult to confirm the opinions of adults who said that the arts are responsible for improved attendance rates at their schools. Perhaps the more compelling evidence is the voices of students themselves who said that their arts programs kept them engaged in school—the fourth grader at Pierce Street, for example, who said that art "inspires me more just to come to school and it just makes it more interesting to learn."

Student claims that the arts are the reason they come to school are particularly meaningful when the students are adolescents who can choose for themselves whether or not they will attend. One of the most powerful stories of the ability of the arts to engage students came from a classroom of English language learners at Central Falls High School, where students and teachers were engaged in an arts integrated unit in partnership with the ArtsLiteracy project at Brown University. During the unit, in which students wrote and rehearsed an original performance based on a novel that they were studying, one student was discovered to be sneaking back into school from suspension to participate in the class. His story was almost a legend among teachers and students participating in ArtsLiteracy projects at the school. It is a symbol for them of the kind of learning experience—and learning community—that they have created through their art.

To succeed, the schools show, schools must enable students not only to develop academically but, in doing so, to use their academic skills to interpret and make sense of their lives, to engage the world in productive ways, and to be contributing members to their communities and the broader society. In the schools, the arts were the context for making these connections and provided a powerful framework in which students engaged in the processes of learning that developed their academic, personal, and social capacities. ■

3

Thinking in the Arts

"Many scholars and experts agree that coping with today's challenges calls for better development of individuals' abilities to tackle complex mental tasks, going well beyond the basic reproduction of accumulated knowledge."

— OECD DESECO PROJECT, *THE DEFINITION AND SELECTION OF KEY COMPETENCIES: EXECUTIVE SUMMARY*[18]

One of the concerns expressed by commentators on public education is that schools may not be doing enough to help students develop capacities for problem solving, critical thinking, and decision making—capacities that will allow them to be lifelong learners and to tackle the challenges they will face in life, school, and work. Arts learning experiences help students develop these capacities. In the arts, students have central and active roles as meaning makers. This role demands that they not only acquire knowledge but that they develop the capacity to reflect on what they're learning and to use it as they interpret and create works of art.

Responding to Art

Students in the schools learned that they make meaning in their interaction with a work of art. We have called this interaction a third space. Artist Paul Klee similarly called it "the space in between," "the space, situation and opportunity, which can open up between...a viewer and an object."[19] In this space, students must learn to experience a piece of art and to make judgments about it

THIRD SPACE: WHEN LEARNING MATTERS

37

using the tools of analysis that they have learned in the relevant art form, along with the insight they bring from their own experience. Making meaning from a work of art is a complex intellectual enterprise. Students learn to imagine things – human relationships, ideas, experiences, materials – from different perspectives as they explore the range of possible interpretations of a painting, play, dance, or song. They develop capacities that allow them to see and think about things in new ways.

A student in the Human Creativity arts program at Central Falls High School explained that she appreciated learning this approach and wished that all teachers were able to bring it into their classrooms. "Teachers should learn how to do it through the artist's way," she said. "Look at everything from all points of view. If you don't see things from different points of view it will be boring, just that's right and that's wrong. With art you can go around the subject. You can curve; make shapes; find new ways to enter in."

A vivid example of students engaging these thinking capacities in the interpretation of art in a classroom occurred at Dyett Academic Center High School in Chicago, where a teaching artist was partnering with a history teacher to teach an integrated music, writing, and history unit called "Hip Hop 101." The students were working toward the creation of their own poems and lyrics and, as part of this project, they were taking time to hone their capacities to analyze the songs and lyrics of other artists.

The teaching artist asked students to identify musicians that they listen to regularly. They chose Tupac Shakur, Jay-Z, Eminem, and Missy Elliott. The students then identified a "positive" song and a "negative" song performed by each artist. The titles were written on the blackboard. They engaged in a probing discussion about the possible meanings of the songs, examining both their lyrics and sounds. They described themes they found in the music including race, violence, sex, family, and friendship. They explored why many of the songs could be interpreted as either positive or negative, and why and how songs may be interpreted by different people in different ways. In their conversations, students often evoked examples from their own lives or ways of thinking about human relationships in their explanation of why they found a particular meaning in a particular song.

The students actively participated in the lesson; they were engaged in reflecting upon, analyzing, and making meaning from the songs. The teaching artist referred to the capacities engaged in arts experiences like this one as "critical thinking." He said, "The arts give students practice in critical thinking," which can help them as they try to make sense of other kinds of information they will encounter in the future. Students, he believes, learn from the arts to approach new information, asking what it means, what do we do with it, and how do we feel about it?

In the context of the integrated Hip Hop 101 unit, the artist helped the students to connect this way of accessing and thinking about new information in the arts to learning in history. He reminded them that it is important to look at the knowledge they acquire in history like they look at art, to examine it from different perspectives, practice seeing it in different ways, and make meaning out of it that connects the new information with their experiences of the world. He told the class, "If we let information be poured into us, without doing the work to decipher it, we're going to be confused. Information is going to be washing over us."

With the teaching artist, the students asked: How does the meaning of history change depending on whose perspective it's seen or written from? What are the explicit and implicit messages in the information that is conveyed and left out in their history text book? They tackled these questions in relation to specific topics they'd been covering in history—the fossil record, migration, evolution, how history has variously portrayed Africa in the rise of world civilizations—as critical consumers of history. The new ideas they began to uncover later became the subject of the poems and lyrics they would write. Their engagements with history were framed by their analysis and creation of works of art.

Thinking about Thinking

What the teaching artist at Dyett Academic Center High School called critical thinking, the National Research Council report, *How People Learn: Bridging Research and Practice*, refers to as metacognitive skills—"strategies" that "can be taught that allow students to monitor their understanding and progress in problem solving."[20] Interestingly, the report gives as an example of metacognition, a disposition exhibited by students in the Hip Hop 101 lesson. "In history," it states, "the student might be asking himself, 'who wrote this document, and how does that affect the interpretation of events?'"[21] In all of the schools, students employ metacognitive skills in the analysis and interpretation of works of art—both the work of other artists and their own. We saw, as in the Hip Hop 101 unit, that integrated arts experiences offered students opportunities to analyze new information in other school disciplines with a similar disposition.

The director of the local gallery in Tupelo, Mississippi, who works with the Pierce Street Elementary School drew attention to the importance of students learning to form their own interpretations of works of art. "You don't have to like it," she tells students, "but if you like it or dislike it, we want to know why, we want you to be able to verbalize to us why you don't like a certain piece or why you do and what it means to you." "I know a Pierce Street student," she said, because of their ability to do this. "They are very savvy in the arts. They have a great command of the language—of how to come in and assess a piece of artwork."

The arts, a second-grade teacher at Newton D. Baker said, have given her students "a better sense of how things are connected. Students try to get messages where they normally would glance at something. Now they are more in-depth as to what they see, and how they feel about it."

Creative Process

Like responding to and interpreting works of art, *creating* original artwork demands sophisticated intellectual engagement from students. The different art forms provide a range of frameworks and tools with which students work, but there is no single set of correct answers nor single prescribed way for assembling technical aspects into a work of art—a poem, a dance, a jazz solo. When students create their own artwork, they must apply their technical abilities in the art form and develop their capacities to try out possibilities, solve problems, and revise toward a final product. They learn to critique and to assess their progress in realizing a work of art that will convey to an audience what they envision. Creating a work of art is a process; students learn to know *how* in addition to knowing *what.*

In an integrated arts lesson taught at Pierce Street Elementary School, fourth-grade students engaged in an interrelated set of activities that exemplified the kinds of capacities that students use as they navigate the process of creating an original work of art and the challenges and possibilities that arise along the way.

Students studied the visual artworks of Pablo Picasso and Romare Bearden and examined the geometric shapes in Picasso's cubist painting and in both artists' collages. They practiced collage techniques and made collages of the colors and shapes suggested to them as they listened to classical music. Bearden, they learned, often listened to music as he worked.

They discussed Bearden's *The Piano Lesson* and Picasso's *Three Musicians. The Piano Lesson*, they concluded, was about learning something new. The teacher asked them to reflect on a time when they learned something new, to write a story about it, and then to draw a picture of that moment.

Students had been reading *Hailstones and Halibut Bones* by Mary O'Neill, a collection of poems about color. Building on their discussions of the poems, the students turned their attention to colors in the two paintings, discussing the use of warm and cool colors. "Romare Bearden once said, 'It'll be grand when I can get colors to walk about the picture like free men,'" the teacher told them. Then studying his *Piano Lesson* with the students she asked, "Let's look at the color yellow. Can you find it as it walks around the painting?"

The next assignment in the sequence was to build on what they had discovered in their exploration of Bearden and Picasso's work and to create their own collages using comparable images, colors, and techniques (see figure 16). The parameters of the assignment were clear, but within them, students were told it was important for them to create their own original work. They should create a piece of art that had a relationship to what they had learned but should not re-create or copy what Picasso or Bearden had done.

Students described the experiences. "We had to do different things and she gave us an example on the board, the three musicians that Picasso drew," one fourth grader said. "And we couldn't do that. So we had to do three whatever. So I did three dogs."

"I did three dancing bears," another fourth-grade student said. "And then we had to write a few paragraphs about our picture," another added.

One of the students called these kinds of activities "experiments." She said that other schools her friends go to "don't experiment as much as, I think, Pierce Street does with things. I think that's the thing that really sets it apart from other schools."

As the gallery director who partners with Pierce Street put it, art "teaches students to be creative problem solvers, and I think that opens up a lot of doors for kids so they know they can think differently."

In Human Creativity at Central Falls High School, the students always have a central role in creating the performances that they do. Human Creativity's director explained, for example, that the program's performance art students study a range of art forms, including traditional forms connected to students' cultures such as Cape Verdean dance and African drumming, but when students mount a show, they never merely reproduce what they've been taught. They interpret, adjust, and re-work it to make it their own. Their teacher called these performance pieces "learned representations," adding that when the students create a performance, there is always "something about the work on all levels that is student produced."

Human Creativity mounts three shows each year. The level of student responsibility for these shows increases until the final one when students take charge of all levels of the production from choreography, writing, and directing, to lighting, staging, and sound. When we visited, students were performing one such show called *The Rhythm in Me*.

fig. 16 Piano Street, collage by De'von, Pierce Street Elementary School

The director had given them the title as a prompt, but from there the students had to give it meaning and create and realize all of the show's numbers — dance, theatrical, musical pieces.

Creating in Collaboration

Students navigate the creative process together in collaborative art forms. At Peter Howell Elementary School in Tucson, for example, an artist from the Arizona Opera Company helped a first-grade class work together to plan and analyze the staging for an opera they had been creating. It was an ordinary room, but the students imagined it to be a theater and had to decide where the stage would be and where their audience should sit. They discussed the characters in their opera and the emotions that they might be feeling and explored how that emotion could be expressed on stage through voice and pantomime. They examined closely the movements of the characters and how the personality of each would be conveyed to the audience. "We can keep track of the characters by the hats they wear," one first grader said. "Can we practice our pantomime with each other?" another asked (see figure 17).

The class was alive with energy, debating, shaping, and performing the emerging new work. They were held together in their collaboration by the shared purpose of creating an opera and expressing their story to an audience through the operatic form. As students brainstormed ideas, they constantly had to analyze and make decisions about how the various ideas would or wouldn't fit together in their opera. Students designed a sequentially ordered plot to tell their story. They reflected on how the opera was taking shape, evaluated alternatives, made judgments and decisions about what would improve the piece, and collaborated in its production.[22] As they brainstormed, the teacher encouraged them to work together to "find the connections," the connections among their different ideas and the connection of new ideas to the story they were trying to bring to life.

The students were engaged in what educational researcher Dennie Palmer Wolf calls, "sustained and coherent collaboration that supports the development of a taste for more than convenient solutions [and] a capacity for understanding complex meanings."[23] In creating original

fig. 17 Students at Peter Howell Elementary School perform an opera.

operas – she reported in *Why the Arts Matter in Education or Just What Do Children Learn When They Create an Opera?* – students progressively develop judgments about how well their work is expressing what they want to say and they find ways to talk to one another about it and to make decisions about how to adjust the work to enhance its quality.

Adaptive Expertise

In analyzing the impact of the arts on the context and conditions for learning in the schools, we were helped by a conversation with cognitive scientist John Bransford about a model he and colleagues, Daniel Schwartz and David Sears, propose to explain how students might develop the interest and ability to apply what they are learning to new situations and experiences in school and in daily life, an ability called "adaptive expertise."[24]

They discuss two important dimensions of learning: one in which students become progressively more competent ("efficient") at the routine procedures or technical aspects of a subject – the steps required to solve math problems, for instance, or, within the arts, to master the playing of scales in music, positioning in dance, drawing in visual art, and the like. Students become more competent at the basic processes and can respond successfully to meet the advanced challenges or problems encountered in a subject or skill area. They work more and more efficiently. The second dimension is when the student is "innovative" and imaginative in approaching a subject, envisioning a range of possible questions, approaches, solutions – thinking outside the box.

Bransford and colleagues propose that when these two dimensions are brought together in a learning experience, a "corridor of optimal adaptability" is created in which students wed innovation and imagination to procedural competence to adapt or design new approaches to learning and action, thus becoming "adaptive experts."[25]

Because the arts are acts of the individual's imagination brought to fruition by the disciplined use of the technical features of the form – the making of a poem, a song, a dance, a play, a painting – they have at their core the marriage of efficiency and innovation embodied in adaptive expertise. The high-quality arts learning experiences that we saw in the schools helped students to develop in both of these dimensions.

According to Bransford and his colleagues, an important quality distinguishing "adaptive expertise" from "routine expertise" is that adaptive expertise "often requires 'letting go' or 'holding lightly' solutions and interpretations that are efficient in other contexts. And, it often involves actively interacting with people, tools, and environments to discover gaps and misalignment in one's knowledge that need to be reconciled as well as gaining access to new structures, interpretations, and forms of interaction."[26]

We saw at the schools that the arts gave students practice in this kind of adaptation and that students were developing a disposition to "hold lightly" to solutions as they responded to the new possibilities that naturally arise in the creative process through the engagement with their medium and the interplay with collaborators in ensemble arts. They also learned to respond to new possibilities shown to them in the reactions of an audience—a teacher's critique, the comments of fellow students, the responses of attendees at exhibits and plays—which helped them to become attuned to ways they could improve their work.

As Elliot Eisner writes, in the arts, "Opportunities in the process of working are encountered that were not envisioned when the work began, but that speak so eloquently about the promise of emerging possibilities that new options are pursued. Put succinctly, surprise, a fundamental reward of all creative work, is bestowed by the work on its maker."[27] In the arts, students must be open to new possibilities. They develop the capacity for what John Dewey calls "flexible purposing," revising the process of creation based on possibilities that didn't exist when the work was started.[28] Through this flexible purposing there is constant movement forward in what Bransford and his colleagues call the optimal corridor toward greater adaptive expertise. In the arts, students are learning to do more than solve routine tasks efficiently; they are learning to adapt to novel situations and to learn.

Demands and Rewards of Ownership

In the arts, students have ownership over the creative process and its products. Ownership demands responsibility. It requires students to be self-directed learners. In bringing their personal artistic vision to fruition, they are the ones who must figure out how to get the work done. In so doing, they develop the capacity to determine realistically where they stand in mastering the skills of the art form, and they set personal goals and expectations for the next stages of growth.

High School students in the Central Falls Human Creativity program said, for example, that they have learned through the demands of putting together theatrical and dance performances how to conceptualize, organize, and balance multiple tasks to get things done and to be prepared for classes and rehearsals. A student described this process: "It was a lot of organization." Another said, "Everything has to be sequentially right" (see figure 18).

Students in the ArtsLiteracy program described a similar appreciation for the responsibility that they have in creating their art. They don't just like the acting and the music that is involved in their classes, they said, but they like "trying to put performances together." They value the organization, teamwork, and problem-solving skills that they develop in the process. "It's hard putting a show together," said one student.

Students learn to monitor their progress in meeting the challenges of the creative process. "The kids are the first to know when [a performance] works," the band teacher at Sheridan Global Arts and Communications School said. "And you can look at them and they know when they've nailed something and they really got it, and they just light up. They know when they've made it work. And they know what they need to do to get there."

"I know I can do better, but I need to practice more," said a student at Peter Howell Elementary School.

"When students have a real audience they are preparing their art for," the director of the ArtsLiteracy project said, "they create a self-imposed set of high standards. They demand a high level of quality from each other and themselves." These self-imposed standards of

fig. 18 Students at Central Falls High School rehearse for a dance performance.

quality motivate students in their work more powerfully than external standards imposed by others.

The ownership over the creative process and resulting works of art give students satisfaction. Though they find the work challenging, it is also highly rewarding. Students at all of the schools described that work in the arts is, to borrow a phrase from mathematician and educator Seymour Papert, "hard fun"—"fun *because* it was hard rather than *in spite* of being hard."[29]

The Contexts and Conditions for Learning

In *How People Learn: Brain, Mind, Experience, and School*, John Bransford and colleagues for the National Research Council synthesized research on the qualities found in learning environments that support the cognitive development of students.[30] Interestingly, in a later report, Milbrey McLaughlin, looking at the characteristics of settings that promote positive youth development, found virtually identical qualities.[31] And, Deborah Stipek and colleagues, reviewing literature on student engagement, also refer to the *How People Learn* report, commenting that the settings that support cognitive development and student engagement are the same.[32]

Together these reports indicate that whether the goal is to foster student cognitive development, personal development, or engagement in learning, school settings should embody the environmental qualities identified in *How People Learn.* Stipek and her colleagues state these qualities succinctly as "active participation," "higher order thinking," "variety," "collaborative activities," and "meaningful connections to students' cultures and lives outside of school."[33]

Strikingly, the list expresses well the environments that the arts open in schools, the contexts and conditions that engage students in learning that matters to them and develops the intellectual and the personal capacities we have described. ■

4

Arts, Literacy, and Communication

"An expanded definition of literacy goes beyond skills to include people's willingness to use literacy.... School literacy should be redefined to highlight... instructional practices that involve an active process of meaning-making, writing instruction that makes students' background experiences central, culturally responsive instruction, and the development of critical literacy."

— KATHERINE AU, *LITERACY IN MULTICULTURAL SETTINGS*[34]

The arts create an environment that is ripe for student learning and development. Teachers can bring non-arts school subjects into this space—to be taught and learned—through integrated instruction. In integrated instruction, students make connections between the content and skills of non-arts and arts disciplines. The learning in the disciplines becomes part of a cohesive experience that happens in the third space opened by the arts, a space in which, as Katherine Au writes, "instructional practices... involve an active process of meaning-making" and "students' background experiences [are] central."

Across the schools, we saw powerful examples of arts integration where the arts were taught in tandem with other school subjects—mathematics, science, history, social studies, and language arts. In this chapter, we focus on the integration of arts and language arts as an example of this kind of integrated instruction. We do so because literacy has become such a central measure of school success, and because literacy and language development are of paramount importance in the ten schools, where mastering English is a formidable challenge for many students.

Students in classes that integrated the arts and language arts learned an art form while developing literacy and communication skills, including an increased desire and ability to comprehend often complex texts – their plot, themes, and characters – and to express orally and in writing thoughtful interpretations of the texts. In this kind of instruction, students also grew in their ability to reflect on and write about their own stories, ideas, feelings, and experiences.

Meaningful Literacy Instruction

An exemplary unit integrating arts and language arts instruction was the Dream Keepers project done at Central Falls High School. Two teachers co-teaching an English language arts class developed this unit working with an artist from the ArtsLiteracy project at Brown University. ArtsLiteracy is an explicit effort to help adolescent students develop their literacy skills in the course of arts experiences.

The teachers working on the Dream Keepers project teach in a classroom of students learning English as a second language, students who have low levels of literacy in both English and their native language. This group of students, the teachers said, has been disenfranchised in the school for a range of reasons including their lack of proficiency in English, disability, or behavioral problems. Others in the school, they said, thought of this class as the last stop for students before dropping out or being expelled.

In the Dream Keepers project, the teachers engaged students in multiple arts experiences, including poetry, music, theater, and visual art. Throughout the project, the teachers and an ArtsLiteracy teaching artist, a puppet master, partnered to support students' work. The project began with an exploration of the theme of dreams in the poetry of Langston Hughes, in the paintings of Marc Chagall, in the music of Miles Davis, in the novel *The Long Way to a New Land* by Joan Sandin, and in students' own lives.

Based on this exploration, students then created their own text and artwork. As is typical of ArtsLiteracy projects, they worked toward a culminating performance, an original performance based on their interpretations of the texts and other works they had studied and the connections they made with their personal stories and experiences. The puppet artist helped the students to create their performance. The students visited him in his studio and learned how he developed and expressed his characters and narratives. They added a visual dimension to their performance by applying techniques they learned from the artist to create puppets of cardboard and paint to bring their characters to life (see figures 19 and 20).

The project embodied many of the dimensions we saw supporting literacy development in other schools for students of all ages. It was connected to students' lives, it actively engaged them, and it allowed them to express themselves and offer a meaningful product to their community.

fig. 19 Central Falls students involved in the Dream Keepers project perform with puppets.

fig. 20 A Central Falls student creates a puppet for a Dream Keepers performance.

Making Students' Experiences Central

Students in the Dream Keepers project found particularly strong connections between their personal stories and those of the characters in *The Long Way to a New Land*, a novel about immigrating to the United States. Many of the students had recently had this experience.

One of the teachers shared with our research team a journal that he kept during the project. In the journal he wrote, "Many strong images began to surface" as the students probed the characters' stories, images with which the students made strong connections. "The image of struggle against great odds, the image of packing one's world of possessions into a suitcase or a trunk, the image of selling one's possessions for a ticket to a new life, of saying good-bye to friends and relatives in anticipation of the journey.... Of enduring hardship and encountering the many dangers and obstacles of the journey to a new land."

The teacher wrote that, more and more, as the students read and acted out the novel together, they interspersed their own stories: "Ruddy told of the two-month journey from Guatemala, on foot and by bus. Moises told of coming to America from El Salvador, by bus and on foot, through the desert and the mountains (see figure 21). Jairo spoke briefly about being left with his grandmother in Colombia at age one and of leaving her to come to the U.S. when he was fifteen." The stories, the teacher wrote, "provided a perspective that took my breath away. These are the stories that they have been waiting to have someone ask them to tell. These are the stories that beg to be written and eventually to be shared and performed."

Doing performance and literacy work that is connected to students' lives is typical of ArtsLiteracy. "We have always done performances that are connected to their personal stories," the teacher said. "It's authentic. It is a unique experience in their lives to find these things valued. And because they are valued and appreciated, there is a greater willingness to put substantially more effort into the process of communicating, orally and in writing."

Students in this classroom said that arts integrated projects, like Dream Keepers, motivated them to tell their stories and to do the hard work of understanding and creating text. They said: "Acting it out; it becomes more fun. You want to stay up and keep reading" (see figure 22). "We didn't want to read before, now we even pick out our own books." "You're accomplishing something, working real hard—you went all the way you didn't quit." "As long as you do the work, you can be whoever you want. Do your work. That's what we do." "I love when we do the work." "We just go to school because of that class" (see figure 23).

The authenticity of the experience in projects integrating the arts and language arts, the teacher said, directly supported students' literacy development from story comprehension to sophisticated interpretations of texts, identification of characters and their motivations, recognition of irony and other literary devices, and the development of expressive language, both written and oral.

"Once the quality of the learning experience has changed," he said, "there's a significant difference in students' level of competence in literacy and language."

fig 21

The American Dream
By Moises, Central Falls High School

On Thursday the twenty-third of January two thousand and three, I left my country, El Salvador for the United States of America. On the twenty-second, I said good-bye to all of my family, and at four o'clock the next morning I took the bus from my home to the capital city, where I arrived at nine o'clock, a little hungry because I had not eaten anything. After walking about a half mile to the East bus terminal in San Salvador, I got on the bus to Guatemala. After about four hours of travels, the bus stopped at the immigration station on the border of Guatemala where the immigration officials stole seventy dollars from me and my cousin.

When we arrived in Guatemala, we left the bus and looked for the "coyote" who was supposed to bring us to America. After a long time, he finally appeared. My cousin told him that she had to give some of the money that she had brought to pay him to the immigration police. He said that he did not care and that if he did not get all of the money, he would not take us to the next place.

It was 11:00 o'clock at night and we still hadn't eaten anything since our journey began at four o'clock in the morning. The "coyote" gave us a cup of coffee and a little bread and brought us to a hotel, where we slept until six o'clock the next morning. We took the bus to La Mesilla, Guatemala which is on the border between Guatemala and Mexico where we stayed for the next two days. We ate very well and I played soccer and saw the girls and listened to music. But I was sad there and I cried for my family.

After two days we left La Mesilla on foot with two other people. We crossed a mountain to the next city. When we arrived there, a car was waiting for us, but we could not cross the street because the police were nearby. Finally, the police were not looking, we ran across the street and got in the car. We had to hide beneath the seats of the car and I had to stay there for two days. After two days, we got on a bus to Mexico. We arrived in Mexico where we stayed for another two days. They moved us by bus to Agua Pietra in Mexico. First I had to pass Immigration, but I tried to speak like a Mexican and the Immigration did not bother me.

We spent twenty-four hours without eating anything traveling to Agua Pietra. Finally the bus stopped at the border between the United States and Mexico. Immigration came on the bus to look at us. Finally, they told us we could get off the bus. There was a

Bronco waiting for us. I was the last one to get in the car. The police stopped us and told us to get out of the car. We didn't have any documents of identification. We were only two meters from the border to the United States and I said to myself, "RUN"! Without stopping, I ran and crossed a dried up creek bed where the others were secretly hiding. We hid there for ten minutes after which the police finally left.

We got up and began walking. After two hours, we were attacked by robbers. They took my jacket and my shoes. I had forty dollars in my shoes, but I took it out fast and buried it about an inch in the ground. One of the robbers told me that if I didn't give him my money and all of my clothes, he would kill me. They put a gun to my head. Today I thank God that I am alive, but if I were dead, I would have rested.

The robbers left us and we continued walking. I was without my jacket and my shoes and I was cold. When we finally arrived to our destination, we saw many other people....The Immigration passed nearby, and we had to hide. At midnight we were still out waiting to cross. We had to stay close together because it was cold. We had to rest because we didn't want to be too tired to cross. We were thirsty, but we found frozen water. Finally, at five o'clock the next morning we crossed the border into Arizona where a car passed by for us. My guide's leg was injured from the crossing, and I helped him a lot.

We stayed in a house in Douglas, Arizona and from there we went to another house in Phoenix. In Phoenix, my mom called me to see if I had arrived safely. She told me that they would send a Salvadoran to get me. He picked me up in a beautiful truck and drove me to Los Angles. She sent money to Los Angles for my airplane ticket to Rhode Island.

When I got on the plane, everyone spoke to me in English. Nobody was Hispanic, only me. They offered me food on the plane, but I did not understand what they were saying. Finally, the plane arrived in Providence. It was night and I was very tired from the long ride.

I hadn't seen my mother in twelve years, since I was four years old. I had only seen her in photos. I did not know if I would recognize her, but I was happy because I was in the United States and because I would soon be with my mother again. My mother saw me, and she knew me right away. She had brought a picture of me and now I am here telling my story.

fig. 22 Central Falls High School students acting in the classroom.

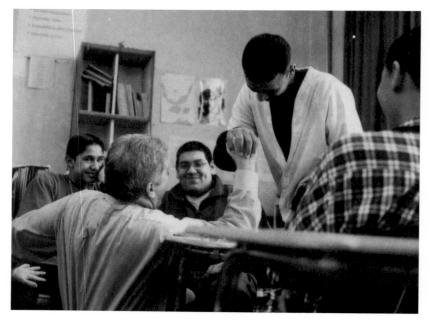

fig. 23 A Central Falls High School teacher congratulates a student on his performance.

ARTS, LITERACY, AND COMMUNICATION

Getting into Character

Each of the ten schools integrated language arts instruction with forms of drama. These forms included, among others, the writing and performance of plays, monologues, and operas. Students and teachers said that an important way in which these experiences enhanced students' literacy skills was their ability to help them better understand characters. Drama creates a safe space in which students are able to get inside the characters in a narrative and develop capacities for understanding their perspectives and motivations.

Students in the Central Falls High School classroom that did the Dream Keepers project said that when they read a new piece of literature together, they use the theater skills that they have developed working with teaching artists from ArtsLiteracy to understand its characters. They read the story aloud with different students taking turns playing different characters in what their teachers refer to as "readers' theater." Performing text, students explained, drives them to try and understand where characters are coming from and what their motivations are because doing so is necessary if they are to play their characters well. As one student said, "When you come out there [on stage] you need to come out there with a purpose. It helps you perform better if you get into the character, knowing their mentality, what they're thinking."

"Students learned a lot about the merits of really studying text and practicing and developing character," a teaching artist said of a unit he did with this class at Central Falls. He worked with them as they studied August Wilson's play, *Fences*, and wrote their own performance based on the play. "I think that performance helped them to understand what the characters [in *Fences*] were going through at that time in their lives, for example being an African-American man in that historical setting, striving to be the first Black driver for his garbage company. I think they learned a lot about history and also I think they made a lot of connections to their own lives." As the students created their performance based on *Fences*, he said, "The specific scenes that we did were the ones that they chose, those scenes that resonated with them. Whether they had to do with specific family things or ideas of being minorities struggling against a system that is not welcoming." A student underlined the point, "We're in every story. Us and them. Us and them."

At Newton D. Baker School of Arts, fifth-grade students mounting an original opera that they wrote with a teaching artist from the Cleveland Opera described a different way in which they got into the characters in their opera. Their opera, called "The Vision of Disaster," was based on their study of Native American culture and history, which was the school's year-long, school-wide theme. Its creation was informed in particular by what they had learned about the Cherokee and Chickasaw tribes and a study of artwork by contemporary Native American artist Beverly Hungry Wolf. The students said that in developing the narrative for the opera, they had to decide how their characters would behave. In making these decisions, the students imagined themselves in the characters' shoes and asked themselves what they would do if they faced the decisions and obstacles that their characters did. They placed themselves in the story and together explored different possibilities, human emotions, and actions.

In their opera, for example, the characters embarked on a long journey because they were running away from a vision that one had had of impending danger. The students needed to decide how the characters would handle the obstacles they encountered in the course of the journey and how their story should end. The central question they debated among themselves was whether their characters would or should return home to face the danger. They tried out a range of possibilities and explained that they learned a lot in doing so. One fifth-grade student, for example, said that she "learned that if you fight, danger won't go away."

In the end, the students communicated through the lyrics of their final number a set of lessons which they had developed and wanted to share with their audience: "I can't believe we ran from danger," the students sang. "We should have stayed and been brave. Maybe the danger was our fear! Maybe it was inside us! You can't run from your problems. You must face your fears. Work to find a solution, or you'll

ARTS, LITERACY, AND COMMUNICATION

be running for years.... After all we've been through, we've learned from our mistakes. We must communicate, to conquer fear and hate!"

Students at P.S. 130 in Brooklyn also said the integrated theater and language arts units that they participated in helped them to learn how to understand stories and characters better. In particular, fifth-grade students described a project in which they wrote original, personal monologues. The project was taught by a teaching artist from ArtsConnection—an external organization that is the school's partner in arts integration—working with their classroom teacher.

"Monologues are like writing a story," one fifth grader said. "It's like you're writing a book. You have to write the setting, the place, where and what does [the main character] want and how is he going to get it. And it's also teaching you to act. You're not just reading; you're actually acting how he acts. It's using your imagination."

A classmate echoed the view: "A monologue helps you by showing you that you have to really develop a character. It's the same thing when you're reading a book, you have to concentrate on the person, look all over and see where he is. If you're reading a book you think what does he want? How is he going to get it and what's his problem? What's stopping him?"

Communication

Students, teachers, and parents said the desire and ability of students to communicate through written and oral language increased as their arts experiences improved their grasp of the significance, structures and processes of language.

A student who participated in the monologue project at P.S. 130 told of her own improvements in writing: "The monologues help me more in my writing," she said. "They made my writing more interesting, because when I write a monologue. I think about cause and effect, and I try to write more details. When [the artist] is not here and my teacher says I have to write a story, I think about what we did [with the artist] and then try to make a story that is more interesting to me."

At Peter Howell Elementary School in Tucson, one of the schools where the students created original operas, teachers said the students working on the operas read more eagerly, read more often, and were highly capable of discussing what they read. One teacher commented on improvements in their writing. They use "big words," she said, especially when expressing their emotions, and they use colorful language when they are trying to describe something.

Peter Howell parents also said that their children's writing became more detailed and descriptive, and showed evidence of a deeper understanding of what they were studying and a growing desire and capacity to articulate it.

A student in the Central Falls High School Human Creativity arts program said, "You can write things differently because you have more expression in your writing."

"Before I would just write because I had to, but now I actually think about what I write and I put what I feel inside," another student said.

Measured Outcomes

School district officials in Tucson and teachers at Peter Howell Elementary credit the school's integrated arts programs for the improved scores of students on Arizona's standardized tests, including improvement in reading and mathematics. District officials commissioned an evaluation that shows that the Opening Minds Through the Arts program used at Peter Howell has had similar effects at other schools in the district. Based on these results, the program is being considered for adoption statewide.

Pierce Street Elementary in Tupelo, Mississippi, makes a similar claim. Pierce Street has the highest number of entering students deemed at risk for failure by the school district's early prevention of school failure assessment, failure that predictably would include performance on standardized reading tests. Yet, school officials said that they dramatically reduce failure rates within the first year or two that students are in the school and were proud of a recent award from the state of Mississippi for the rate of improvement of their students on state exams. Their arts programs, they believe, engage students in learning activities that are meaningful to them, and help them to master a range of literacy skills required by the different art forms and applicable to the material on the standardized tests.

Hand Middle School in Columbia, South Carolina, was equally proud of its test results, particularly the eighty-five percent rate of improvement in the scores of its African-American students, who make up half of the student body. Hand had also been named an Exemplary Writing School by the Writing Improvement Network and South Carolina Department of Education.

Literacy, the schools have found, is advanced by a desire to understand, master, and use the multiple forms of human communication to grasp matters deeply and to express personal meanings. Creating works of art, which inherently calls for a personal stamp, seems uniquely powerful in generating the commitment to acquiring the skills to do so. Ultimately, students are helped to learn to read, speak, and write with skill and enthusiasm when to do so matters to them. ■

5

When Teaching Matters

"Powerful teachers are strengths-based and student-centered. They use students' own experiences, strengths, interests, goals, and dreams as the beginning point for learning, competence, and accomplishment. Thus, they tap students' intrinsic motivation, their existing, innate drive for learning."

— BONNIE BENARD, *RESILIENCE: WHAT WE HAVE LEARNED*[35]

Six students in a high school classroom at Central Falls finished a series of drama warm-up exercises and took turns reading aloud poems, stories, and rap lyrics they had written. They were preparing for a school performance. "Come out more" the teacher encouraged each of them, suggesting gestures and vocal techniques to add personality and life to their reading. The class was respectful and attentive, murmuring support and appreciation as each student worked to refine a presentation.

A young man completed his poem. He confessed he is always nervous about reading in public. He thinks about all of the eyes that will be staring at him. But he has found a technique to help him. He imagines the eyes "as stars twinkling out there."

The rhythm of the class continued and the presentations grew stronger. There was a rustle at the back of the room. Several adults had come in and were looking for something, talking among themselves as they searched.

The teacher turned to them and gestured for them to leave. "We are involved in something important here," he told them.

Teachers are key in determining how meaningful the arts will be to students. They unlock the capacity of the arts to engage students when they treat student works of art as an emerging expression of something very personal, a risky revelation of ideas, emotions, and experiences that are deeply felt.

This attitude, demonstrated by the Central Falls High School teacher, creates the kind of environment for engaged and active learning we are calling third space—a space with an impact on teachers as well as on students. It fosters a spirit of exploration, an enthusiasm for learning, a "we are in this together" feeling among students and teachers, a mutual agreement that "we're involved in something important here." Establishing that climate promotes a willingness in students to do the hard work of learning. For many of the students we met at Central Falls and at the other case study schools, school has often been a place of failure and frustration and the experience of success in the arts is a revelation; learning can matter; they matter. Teachers unleash that potential by the way they treat students' work.

Artists and the teachers whose teaching has been transformed through partnership with an artist create a classroom environment in which students, as one Central Falls student said, get to share who they are and "where they're coming from." These classrooms stand in contrast to other classrooms, he explained, where teachers "don't care about our needs; they just don't care about where we're coming from, they just don't get it" (see figure 24).

Learning from Artists

To unleash the potential of the arts to create a strong environment for learning in their classrooms, teachers needed to have a deep understanding of the nature of work in the arts. Without this understanding they were unlikely to take the students' artwork seriously in all its dimensions—to grasp the intellectual and emotional processes it engaged and the meanings it expressed.

Some of the non-arts teachers in the schools had a personal background in the arts to draw on in supporting and responding to student artwork. Other teachers needed to acquire skill and comfort with the arts and had developed or were developing these capabilities through their schools' arts programs. They participated in a range of arts learning experiences from professional development workshops to ongoing arts lessons. These experiences were most effective for teachers when they provided the opportunity to partner with practicing artists in their classrooms – teaching artists or the school's arts specialists – to develop the kind of arts integrated units described throughout this book.

In order to bring the influence of artists into classrooms, schools created opportunities for classroom teachers to have common planning time with the school's arts specialists and in some cases structured schedules and staffing so that arts specialists and classroom teachers could co-teach integrated units. The most common strategy among the schools, however, was to bring in teaching artists from the surrounding community to partner with classroom teachers to develop and deliver arts integrated units (see figure 25).

All of the schools had community partners – an orchestra, theater, museum, university, arts agency – that helped place teaching artists in the schools. Partnerships with these teaching artists were an important and often crucial catalyst for creating new dynamics in the schools. They brought to the classrooms their advanced skills in the art form and also their own experiences of personal growth and development fostered by their careers in the arts. As artists they knew it didn't come easily, that art was hard and challenging work. They modeled for classroom teachers respect for the struggle of the students to reveal themselves in their works and also how to encourage and help students master the processes of the relevant form to enable them to more fully realize the goals of the integrated lesson.

A Dyett Academic Center High School student participating in an integrated poetry, photography, and English unit – a collaboration between his English teacher and a Columbia College artist – said, for example, "We learn a lot more" with the arts integrated units. The artist

fig. 24

Becoming of Age
By Natasha, Central Falls High School

Becoming of age
    in a world of high egotistical
    well-read folks watching us lay in a heap of demise
    who won't allow me to be me!

    Who struggles?
    You struggle.
    We struggle.
    I know I struggle
    to receive the standardized education
    in order to expand the scope of my brainpower,
    the intellect that comes with my lyrical soul

To receive trust
    So I can distinct the difference
    Between
    Love...
    Infatuation
    And yes of course Lust

    I need teachers who will teach
    Instruct edify and train;
    Guide my slightly composed path
    So future light can shine upon me.

    With a teacher's keen love
    I'm going to be
    the beautiful tree
    standing free
    representing me.

    Education.
    I want to be educated.
    This is what I need,
    not what I want.
    Because truly what I want is not what I need.

    So who will help?

    Teacher?
    Mama?
    Principal?

Disagree with me.

Up yonder lays the dragon tree
ablaze in spicy, scorching flames.

Burn I must not.
As you see
I have a lot
of learning.
I'm simply rising.
I need...
        Influence,
        Control,
        Direction
        Aim,
        Navigation,
        Respect,
        Affection
        Regard...

Teacher...
It's you I need!

fig. 25 Teachers and teaching artists plan a unit at P.S. 130.

"likes poetry so it's easier than when somebody is just telling you something and they haven't experienced it, right? They're just telling you, but she's reading us her poetry that she wrote; then she can explain it to us."

Enlightened Teaching

Classroom teachers learned new attitudes and skills from their collaborations with teaching artists or with school arts specialists. They realized that in teaching the arts they need to be not just instructors who provide information, but facilitators (see figure 26). They have to support students in creating original and imaginative works, works in which students make connections between what they already know and the new knowledge and skills they are acquiring.

A Dyett Academic Center student said that teachers with this attitude are "good teachers." They "like to listen to what students have to say, not just think that they're supposed to tell us this and that just because they're the teacher."

Teachers learned to encourage and give permission to students to express themselves in their art, and they described learning about students through their artwork as an illuminating and important outcome of the arts integrated units in their classrooms. The works that emerged made visible students' backgrounds, understandings, and skills that often had been hidden, allowing teachers to see how they could build on what students knew and to engage them more actively in learning. This outcome was particularly important because the students in the schools often had to struggle to reconcile their cultural backgrounds with the expectations of teachers and the school.

The director of the ArtsLiteracy Project that works with teachers and artists at Central Falls High School said, "A lot of these kids in this school are behind curtains of various kinds. You just don't know who they are; you, as a teacher, have no idea where they are, and if you don't find ways to get them to embody, physically, their learning, you're not going to be able to have any sense of where they are socially, or cognitively, or academically. The arts allow kids to really embody and make their learning visible in a variety of ways."

fig. 26

Teaching Poetry
By Will, teaching poet, Grizzly Hill School

Poetry, like passion, like insight, can not be taught. Yet it must be learned. I motivate, enthuse and am a co-participant in a creative process that defies empirical sequential concepts or explanations. Here is a strong group dynamic at work, simultaneously with the most personal and private inner searching. We work together as poets and sometimes when we share, the poems give us goosebumps and a tingling up our spine. I make a safe place for them to share, provide openings from which to start, encourage them and assume the high worth of their creation. They do the rest.

The revelation is mutually beneficial to teachers and students. In *How People Learn: Bridging Research and Practice*, the National Research Council reports, "Students come to the classroom with preconceptions about how the world works. If their initial understanding is not engaged, they may fail to grasp new concepts and information presented in the classroom, or they may learn them for the purposes of a test, but revert to their preconceptions outside the classroom."[36] "Teachers must pay close attention to the knowledge, skills and attitudes that learners bring into the classroom," the report states. "This incorporates the preconceptions regarding subject matter, but it also includes a broader understanding of the learner."[37]

In the case study schools, teachers treated the backgrounds and experiences—"knowledge, skills and attitudes"—that students brought to class as assets to be embodied in a work of art, providing insights for the teacher to build on.

A fourth-grade teacher at P.S. 130 told of her own revelation. A young girl had been placed in her classroom in the second half of the school year, and the teacher saw little chance she could fit into the ongoing school work; the girl had just arrived in Brooklyn from Haiti and spoke no English. The class was in the midst of a storytelling project and students were taking turns acting out the characters that appeared in the narrative; one character was a dancing fish. They took turns at it, but the newcomer was the best, and was greeted, the teacher said, with wild excitement and enthusiasm by her new classmates. She was voted "best fish" and would play the role in later performances. She had instant standing in the class the teacher said, in her own eyes and those of the other students; she became part of the community in the classroom.

Another teacher in the school explained a similar value for his partnerships with theater artists. Through the work they did, he said, "I've learned a lot about the kids and that's the big thing. I see them break out of their shell and all of a sudden the cat is out of the bag."

As the principal at P.S. 130 said, "Part of what's so exciting about the arts is that some of the kids who pose the biggest concerns, you tap into something they can do well and then when you see them doing something really well, you think differently about them. It just helps you figure out what your work is, what you've got to do, how to move them forward."

An artist who teaches at Sheridan Global Arts and Communications School explained similarly: "I think that the [arts] projects bring out teachers' understandings of students in different ways because if there is a student who can never sit still in class and they're given something that engages them, suddenly the teacher understands the student more."

The same artist said that the arts allow students to "learn through different intelligences" and that teachers are sometimes surprised by how the arts engage students, and even *which* students they engage. When a school group comes to her studio, she said, "A teacher will tell me 'watch out for Kenny, he's the one. He won't be able to finish the project; I'll pull him as soon as he starts misbehaving.' And I never know who Kenny is. I'll never know because he's engaged in a different way than he is in the classroom and he's thinking with his hands, with his whole body."

A fourth-grade teacher at Sheridan explicitly uses the arts to get to know her students at the beginning of the school year. She has her students create personal mandalas — the circular forms with symbolic images best known for their use in Buddhist rituals — to express matters of personal significance. The students create icons, images that symbolize things that are important to them, and place them in patterns within their mandalas. They provide keys to explain what the symbols stand for. When we visited near the beginning of the school year, the students' mandalas were hanging in the hallway outside their fourth-grade classroom. The images in the mandalas represented such things as love, trust, nature, math, school, and art.

One fourth-grade student explained what the personal mandala project was about. She said that "the mandala is for the teacher to understand us better." Another fourth grader agreed, "They're trying to get to know you" (see figure 27).

Educational researchers Dick Corbett and Bruce Wilson, who have conducted extensive studies of teaching in urban schools, contend that fundamental to effective teaching and learning is an unqualified conviction on the part of teachers that every student can learn and that it is the responsibility of the teachers to construct the conditions and instructional approaches within which the students will succeed.[38] Generally,

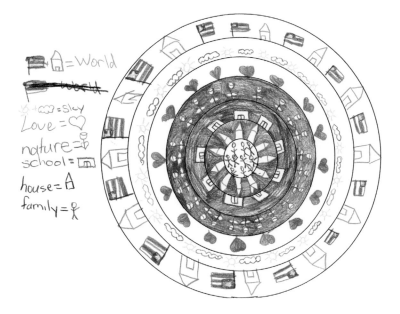

fig. 27 Personal Mandala, drawing by PaShia, Sheridan Global Arts and Communications School

teachers and administrators in the schools we visited shared the belief that all students can learn; it is, after all, a commonplace of educational rhetoric. But they reported that through their school arts programs they were progressively able to remove qualifiers to that belief—able to set aside the "buts" of such perceived obstacles as students' home conditions, language, disability, lack of discipline—as the students revealed themselves more fully in their art making. Teachers more energetically shouldered the responsibility laid on them by Corbett and Wilson as they discovered the individuality and capabilities of their students and found the instructional approaches that worked best in their classrooms. They felt more successful, and therefore more fulfilled, in their teaching.

Teacher Satisfaction and Renewal

The principal at Grizzly Hill on the San Juan Ridge in California said that "the arts are contagious" because of the confidence, expression, and engagement that they foster among students, but also because of "the effects they have at the staff level." He said, "Good teachers want to see authenticity in their students, want to see them engage with what they're learning." He finds that the arts do this and so help to increase teachers' professional satisfaction.

Indeed, teachers in the case study schools said they derive delight and professional renewal and satisfaction from incorporating the arts into their teaching. They enjoy teaching more, primarily because of the responsiveness of their students and the new level of collaboration with other teachers in the school. Dissatisfaction with teaching is an enormous problem in public schools across the country. More than fifty percent of all new teachers quit within the first five years in the classroom.[39] In contrast, the enthusiasm for teaching reported by teachers in these schools was striking and encouraging.

A teacher at Pierce Street Elementary School in Tupelo, Mississippi said teaching has become "a lot more fun; the kids pay more attention, and it keeps me awake too, especially since I teach science and social studies and math. The students pay more attention and they're more interested in what we're doing if we incorporate art instead of just reading off notes or

WHEN TEACHING MATTERS

just doing a pencil and paper activity. To me, they relate to it more, and you're getting to move around, you're getting to do something, you're not just sitting strictly at a desk all day long, you get to actually move and you hit all those learning styles. I even learn things having to teach this."

These comments echo the findings of a recent study by arts researcher Barry Oreck of the attitudes of classroom teachers who are involved in integrated arts programs. The teachers reported that they are motivated to take on the often challenging task of increasing their competence in an art form as part of their teaching because of the insights the arts give them into the individual differences of their students and the increased satisfaction that it provides them as teachers.[40]

As a teacher at Central Falls High School explained, integrating the arts can be "a lot more work." "But," she said, "I don't really care how hard you have to work if it works. It takes longer, but there are deeper things that come out of it."

Teachers said that exploring with their students the interrelationships among different disciplines in the arts integration programs made sense to them on a very basic level. It fits the way they believe students operate in the world outside of school, where the boundaries of disciplines are more fluid and the challenge is to create an integrated understanding of how the world works (see figure 28).

As a teacher at Hand Middle School put it, the nature of the child itself is an integrative force. Children, she said, are multidimensional and multi-talented, and "arts integration hooks into that." "They don't see the world in compartments. The conscious connection was immediate for the children."

The Challenge of Change

The transition to an arts-integrated curriculum was not always easy for teachers. The process of change could be difficult, even when teachers partnered with teaching artists and saw greater opportunities to reach students.

Dyett Academic Center High School was in the early phases of implementing integrated arts programming when we visited. A veteran

fig. 28

LEARNING SHOULD BE ALIVE, LIVING AND BREATHING, LIKE WE ARE.
By Deanna, teacher, Central Falls High School

Learning doesn't happen between 4 walls. It happens between people. Teachers should not only be facilitators, but also lifelong learners, letting their students have a turn at guiding them. Schools should not live within the borders of Monday through Friday 8:00 am to 2:30 pm. Schools should be responsible institutions; responsible for educating, responsible for creating a positive and supportive culture, responsible for reaching out, pulling in, taking hold, and letting go. Schools should be the great collaborators of our communities; fostering global thinking, and global understanding.

SCHOOLS SHOULD OFFER HOPE.

English teacher who worked with a teaching artist in a poetry lesson had conflicting feelings about the program.

He recognized that the teaching artist was able to engage his students to an unusual degree: "[The artist] relates well with the kids and gets the kids motivated and raises expectations," he said. "She brings to the table the opportunity for kids to all have a chance to succeed at an interesting project."

The teacher had worked with the artist to develop a unit in which students studied English language skills—particularly writing—in conjunction with photography and poetry. The artist taught the students about photography and took them to a photography exhibition. "We went down to the museum," the teacher said, "and I've never seen a kid so conscientious, so well-mannered, so well-behaved, so receptive; very, very impressive."

The students then created their own photographic images exploring and documenting their daily lives and their communities and wrote poems about their images. What made the unit so engaging, the teacher said, was its personal meaning to students. In writing their poems they "analyzed the visual images *they* created." The unit, he said, was "an attempt to get the kids to mirror and visualize and to be able to express their inner selves."

"I think giving them a chance to step back and analyze what they're doing is something that works well with them, and it gives them an eagerness to show what they've got and what they can become and what they can do," the teacher said. "It gives them an area in which they can feel comfortable and have success. They'll take that with them when they get out of school next year, because they're seniors now."

The teaching artist created a powerful space for learning which stayed open in the classroom when she was gone as students worked with their teacher on writing assignments connected to their photography project (see figure 29). "[The artist] wasn't here," the teacher said, but "the kids again participated almost 100 percent and really dug into themselves." The teacher, however, wasn't fully confident in his ability to sustain this space in the artist's absence. Ironically, what gave him some discomfort with the experience was its very power and his inability to maintain full

fig. 29

Community
By Jeresa, Dyett High School

what used to be our hood
will soon be gone
whites are moving in
one by one
blacks are moving out
two by two

things are changing
no more slanging and hanging
I am going to feel all alone
because my hood
will soon be gone

no more breaking down doors
just back and forth to the stores
no more drug dealing or stealing

just a place with peace and harmony

control of the classroom. "As a matter of fact," he said, "it got actually probably more emotional than we would have liked, because they began expressing their inner feelings and emotions, sometimes being insensitive to feelings of others, and it almost became a little too personal. But, that's good in a sense that they were really digging deep within themselves. So, it was good. It was fine. I think they'll be fine." "It was more than what we expected," he added, "and I think when you get a group of kids involved and focused on a project like that, it's generally a good thing, almost always a good thing, because it's really hard to get some of these kids engaged in much of anything" (see figure 30).

His comments pointed to a possible paradox of introducing quality arts experiences into schools: they can have a profound and emotional impact on students, disturbing the controlled and regimented teaching found in many classrooms. Teaching artists, arts specialists, and some classroom teachers have experience that allows them to engage

fig. 30

Education
By Swazi, Dyett High School

I'm a little black girl in the hood
That's who I be
Let go of these chains
So I can be free

I need my education
And so do you
I need books, papers
And pens too

I will get my education anyways
Whether you like it or not
I'm going to be the one
Who likes to shop

I want to be successful
Like everyone else
I need my education
To care for myself

arising student emotions and channel them into creative expression in the arts, to bring about a third space. However, some teachers may need the regular involvement and support that comes through partnering with an artist to become effective at doing so.

Support for Change

When Barry Oreck asked teachers in his study what made it possible for them to take the risk of embracing the arts as part of their teaching, they told him it was the quality of staff development that was provided; adequate time to work with others to plan and practice new skills; and, crucially, the support and encouragement of their direct supervisors – in most cases, the school principal.[41]

Teachers in the case study schools described this support in various ways and many adopted the language of the arts to describe the change in the school environment. They reported that they are allowed to be "creative." They, like their students, felt they were treated as "artists" who had something uniquely important to contribute within and beyond the curriculum content that they deliver.

"That's the important part of the culture here," a Sheridan Global Arts and Communications teacher said. "The staff is allowed to be creative. And that's not to say we aren't held accountable to our district standards and state mandates and techniques and protocols and all those kinds of things. But we are given a lot of leeway within parameters. We can be creative here."

This sounded to us very much like the model for developing adaptive expertise proposed by Bransford and his colleagues discussed earlier: become efficient at the required and basic methods and procedures and yoke that competence to innovative and imaginative exploration.[42] Teachers report that the freedom and encouragement from school authorities to be creative is an affirmation of their value as individuals and as professionals. Under these conditions, a set of interrelationships comes into play to create energized and successful teaching and learning, a positive setting for learning that moves students and teachers to new levels of success and satisfaction.

The former principal of Sheridan Global Arts and Communications School, who led the transition to an arts-centered school, said that valuing the individual potential and contributions of teachers and students was centrally important to the school's structure and way of delivering instruction as she envisioned it. "I think it's a respect for and valuing of individuality. And you can see that with the [student] artwork and the pieces of work in the portfolios and the writing. And it's also valuing the staff as well. So it's not just one-sided. We value the strengths of the staff."

The principal at Clarkton School of Discovery said, "Traditional teaching is not the status quo here. I think arts integration enables teachers to look for new and different ways to think about presenting traditional goals and objectives. I think children benefit because they see such a variety of teaching techniques and strategies. I think the teachers here are risk-takers."

Teacher Collegiality

Another kind of support important to the teachers was working side by side on a regular basis with their colleagues as they planned and worked on integrated arts projects. Teachers said that these ongoing collaborative experiences enabled them to become progressively more comfortable and competent integrating the arts into their classes. Through these experiences they also forged strong professional relationships.

Bonnie Benard points to the importance of these relationships: "We...know that when teacher collegiality is encouraged and thrives, students achieve better academically." She adds that "structures that support this collegiality include team teaching, reflective practice groups, peer support groups, and peer problem solving groups."[43] These structures were an important part of the arts programming at each of the schools.

"[Arts integration] has brought the faculty together," a teacher at Pierce Street Elementary School said, "and this faculty, when I first came here, was very competitive. Because of our grade level and cross-grade level planning for arts integration, our teachers meet at least once a week. They all have the same time every day free and that has brought our staff together and put everybody on the same page."

Cooperation and respect among the arts specialists and the classroom teachers in the case study schools was an important indicator of such collegiality. Often in schools, arts specialists are isolated from regular school activities, peripheral to their major purposes and goals. This was not the case in the ten schools. At Pierce Street Elementary School a teacher said, "The arts specialists plan with the classroom teachers. You can see the collaboration." At Hand Middle School, where an art teacher had recently been named teacher of the year, the principal said that the arts specialists were the bridge builders assisting teachers in other subjects to work in partnership with arts organizations and artists from the community. A visual arts teacher at Newton D. Baker said, "I never felt that I was a valuable asset to a school until I came here; the classroom teachers here *do* value the arts."

At Sheridan Global Arts and Communications School, a teacher said that the shared sense of purpose and collegiality is visible "in all different levels of the school, all the way from the kids up to the building engineers." She elaborated, "The engineers even are very patient with our messes and our projects, our work in progress that's sitting out day after day and a big mess. And they can't do their work because our stuff takes up so much space. It's really a kind of cooperation that's systematic that our kids had never seen before."

One of Sheridan's arts coordinators agreed that the arts are a unifying force at the school. Art, she says, "It's everywhere. The women in the lunchroom will help us store the pulp [for paper making]. Everybody is on board. We couldn't do that papermaking stuff if the engineers hated the fact that we were getting water on the floor or wouldn't lend us their buckets and all that stuff. The other day, I was carrying buckets of pulp down to the [the room where students make paper] and there was a new engineer and an engineer from last year. And the new engineer made some comment because it was like 'what's that?' And the old engineer went 'ahh' and explained it to him. It's cool."

An important byproduct of the growing collegiality at the schools, as well as the value that supervisors place on teachers' professional work, is an increase in teacher satisfaction. This satisfaction is evident not only in the way in which teachers talk about their work but in a reduction in teacher turnover reported to us at eight of the ten schools.

"Staff turnover at the school and absenteeism is much less than it was when I first started working here, especially staff turnover," a Sheridan teacher reported. "Because people who come here really like working here. As someone who has been here a long time myself, I think we can all see the value of continuity within the staff, teachers who have stayed in the program, staying here and working towards goals that we all understand."

Creating the Conditions for Quality Arts Integration

Classroom teachers collaborating with artists or arts specialists in the schools became both teachers and learners, sharing their content area expertise while developing an understanding of an art form and discovering new capacities for learning in their students and in themselves.

There were teachers in all of the schools who had been resistant to the idea of arts integration when it was first introduced. Both they and school administrators said that the most powerful way to convert reluctant teachers was to engage them directly in arts integration at professional development seminars or workshops, so they could move beyond talk about the arts and have arts experiences comparable to those of students. Teachers also began to change their attitudes through what they called "grassroots transmission," catching wind of the arts integrated lessons happening in other classrooms and observing the effects on students they themselves were struggling to reach. "When they start to see the success that the other classrooms are having, that drives more people in," an artist teaching at Sheridan Global Arts and Communications School said.

A teacher at Newton D. Baker agreed that it is imperative that teachers have a chance to see quality arts integration in practice. She herself had been resistant to the idea and initially refused to become involved in the school's arts programs. But, the impact it was having on students in other classrooms changed her mind. Once they see what it can do, she said of reluctant teachers, "They will be won over."

A veteran teacher at P.S. 130 told of her own experience of being won over. "I was the first to start [arts integration] with my class," she said. But, she explained, her attitude when an artist came into her classroom was: "You're not coming into my room and telling me how to teach my kids. I know what I have to do. You're not with them all day; you leave and then what do I do with them? You're moving my desk around and you're taking all my organization out of my hands; and then I have to deal with this—not realizing that children learn so much more and it's so much easier for them to learn cooperatively. I mean I never dominated a class, I always interacted, but on my terms, not on their terms. And I had to let that go; it now had to be on their terms. And that's hard to do, the transition is very difficult, but once you do it, there's no going back anymore because you see the success that it gives the kids."

She also told of a similar change in a colleague: "We have one particular teacher that I always think about. He comes to my mind because we're around the same age bracket and he's the same kind of structured teacher that I am, or I was. I'm not anymore. I remember when he first had [a teaching artist partner] who dealt with clay." When the artist first came to his classroom, she said, "He would sit and watch and think, 'well I can't do that.' And then the following year, he actually had his hands elbow-deep in the clay, making and doing. By participating he developed a feeling of being able to contribute, which he never thought he could. It's wonderful. I think he now enjoys the arts in a totally different way that he never expected to happen."

There was an initial hesitancy to embrace arts integration among some of the teaching artists as well. An artist working with Sheridan teachers, said, for example, "I'm trained as an artist. I teach art at a college. The idea of arts integration is something that I had to learn to embrace because my initial reaction was that the arts in and of themselves are valuable. And I get a little anxious about 'well we're teaching math through art.' No, the *art* itself is, and that's something that I've learned to understand. The art coexists with the other subject and is extremely important in and of itself. And that's something that I think I always try to bring to the table. And that's something that came most easily to me as a practicing artist. I am a big proponent for what happens in this school because I've experienced it. The quality of life here is very rich because the arts are in there with science and reading and all of it."

Professional Development

Well-constructed professional development programs were critical to teachers' and artists' acceptance of the value of arts integration. Where the schools and their community partners provided opportunities for teachers and artists to explore the theories and practices of arts integration and where adequate time was provided for the joint planning of lessons and experiences for students, the effects could be seen in the classrooms. Cooperation and an enthusiasm for learning was palpable, as was a respectful and easy relationship among students, teachers, and artists, different in kind from most classrooms.

Under the best circumstances, the artists and teachers were provided the time and the conditions to get to know one another and to plan how they would work together with their students. Through these experiences teachers could develop skills in the arts that enabled them to engage students in understanding and demonstrating substantive connections between the art form and another subject, even when the teaching artist or specialist was not with them.

We saw such successful programs in each of the schools, but we also saw cases where time, support, and arts learning opportunities were insufficient to enable classroom teachers to develop adequate skills or confidence to create quality arts learning experiences for their students. Arts activities in classrooms under these circumstances could add a visual activity, a use of music, or physical movement to enliven the classroom experience for students, but it was not clear that students were developing real understanding or ability in the art form. The arts-related activities were not treated as serious work or expressions of self or learning. They were adjuncts to, rather than integral features of teaching and learning.

A teacher at Newton D. Baker School of Arts said that there are two aspects of professional development programs that help teachers develop competence and comfort with arts integration. The best professional development programs, she said, include opportunities for teachers to participate in the types of arts experiences that they would use in their classrooms, and also include analyses of a theoretical framework within which the arts are related to other disciplines. At Newton D. Baker, for instance, she says all teachers and administrators are trained in the concepts and practices of a program developed by the former Getty Education Institute for the Arts in Los Angeles called Discipline Based Arts Education – or DBAE. According to this approach, to understand fully or to make a work of art, the student must bring the disciplines of aesthetics, history, culture, and criticism to bear – learning how the work is made, what it means, how it embodies historical and cultural information and values, and how it is to be judged.

Another framework is that of the integrated ArtsLiteracy program at Central Falls High School. At the core of ArtsLiteracy is a framework designed at the Brown University Education Department. This framework, mentioned earlier, is called the performance cycle (see figure 31). The performance cycle moves teachers and students through a process that begins with building community and proceeds through entering, comprehending, creating, rehearsing, revising, and performing text. Extensive reflection supports the work throughout all its stages.

The most common framework in the schools was an analysis by teachers and artists or arts specialists of the goals of the subject areas that they would integrate. In this process, they would work from the state or local school district standards in the disciplines. The standards for fourth-grade history, for instance, would be compared to those for fourth-grade visual arts and the curricula mapped to find connections, points where integrated activities could address standards in both disciplines and allow students to see meaningful connections between them.

One of the arts coordinators at Sheridan described a professional development program that epitomized the high-quality experiences teachers said were essential. "One of the most recent things we did was bring the entire staff, eighty people, over to the Minnesota Center

BUILDING
COMMUNITY

PERFORMING
TEXT

ENTERING
TEXT

REFLECTION

REHEARSING/
REVISING TEXT

COMPREHENDING
TEXT

CREATING
TEXT

fig. 31 The ArtsLiteracy Performance Cycle developed by Kurt Wootton and Eileen Landay

for Book Arts. They had a whole hands-on morning where they were making books and having a workshop themselves. And we were up there talking about getting some art historians from St. Thomas [University] in to do some work with teachers on arts and African art history that we feel would really be great for the kids and get the teachers on board with that. But we approach it as not just 'here's how to put it in your curriculum,' but 'here you are as an intelligent person. Here's an expert from our community. We want you to have this experience and then use it, as you will. We believe you'll use it well.'"

The book artist who helped lead the teacher workshop said: "It was really exciting. Sheridan has such a strong reputation in the arts in this community. So I was a little intimidated by this group of people who came over. But it was a very engaging day for myself and for my staff and also to see the teachers and actually the whole staff from Sheridan collaborating on projects and brainstorming together. It was a great day to get staff thinking together about how they can use the resources that are already started at the school. So it really was about deepening relationships."

Similar high-quality professional development is offered by the staff of the ArtsLiteracy project who support arts integration at Central Falls High School. ArtsLiteracy brings teachers and artists together over the summer for workshops in which they replicate the experiences they will provide to students over the school year. Teams of artists and teachers work with a text to explore its story, themes, and characters through dramatic activities, and like students in the program, create and perform an original production.

The puppet artist we saw at Central Falls and a teacher and student from the school joined the ArtsLiteracy staff as trainers in a workshop we observed. They led the participating teachers and artists through the same process experienced by students in the Dream Keepers project described earlier. They analyzed a text, wrote an original performance, and mounted the performance using puppets that they had designed and painted collaboratively (see figures 32 and 33). A teacher in the workshop

fig. 32 Teachers and artists paint during an ArtsLiteracy workshop.

fig. 33 Teachers and artists perform during an ArtsLiteracy workshop.

said afterward that an important factor in the experience was the opportunity for teachers to be immersed in arts processes and to participate in the kind of learning community they and partnering artists would create for students in their classrooms during the school year.

Teachers as Learners

At Sheridan Global Arts and Communications School and at Peter Howell Elementary School, classroom teachers take lessons from school arts specialists before or after school to advance their skill in

WHEN TEACHING MATTERS

the arts. At Sheridan, for example, twenty teachers were taking lessons from the strings teacher, and at Peter Howell, teachers were studying violin alongside students in lessons offered by the school's music teacher before school and taking recorder lessons with their own students during music class.

Teachers at both schools reported that their arts lessons have helped them relate better to their students. A teacher who was struggling to learn the recorder at Peter Howell said that for her the experience was a reminder of the challenges her students face when they are learning something new. It enabled her to be more understanding of her students' academic development and empathetic when they encountered obstacles or frustrations. The music teacher at Peter Howell said that "students delight in helping their classroom teachers overcome musical challenges while learning new recorder songs."

A teaching assistant who takes violin lessons at Sheridan commented on the value for students in seeing teachers struggling to learn an instrument. The shared learning experience, she believes, helps students identify with teachers and see that even teachers have things to learn. "I am a role model in my violin lessons," she said, "because the students see that even at this late stage of my life, I'm right where they are. It's good for them to see that you're never too old to learn, that learning is a continual process."

A special education teacher at Central Falls High School found that her students saw her in a new light as they watched her apply the techniques she was learning from the teaching artist with whom she partnered. This was particularly important to her because her students stay with her for the duration of their high school careers. "[H]aving an artist in the room makes a difference," she explained, "because my students have me for four years. They put you in a role. I mean, they see you as this and this and this. And, so, when they see you working with an artist, they start to see you as something different. They say, oh my God, she can do that. They say, I'll trust you."

Imagining Success

The new qualities of teaching and learning in the case study schools are rooted in a nurturing of the imagination. As philosopher Maxine Greene writes, "Imagination is as important in the lives of teachers as it is in the lives of their students, in part because teachers incapable of thinking imaginatively or of releasing students to encounter works of literature and other forms of art are probably also unable to communicate to the young what the use of imagination signifies. If it is the case that imagination feeds one's capacity to feel one's way into another's vantage point, these teachers may also be lacking in empathy."[44] "It takes imagination to break with ordinary classifications and come in touch with actual young people in their variously lived situations."[45]

As a teaching artist at Sheridan said, "I think the arts enrich every one of us. I think that it helps us as adults stay more flexible. And I think that that's just kind of a built-in piece, kind of a whole orientation." ■

6

Building Community

"Though most principals, superintendents, and teachers have a desire to do better and are working as hard as they can to provide a quality education to every student they serve, the road is rough and the going is slow. The lead villain in this frustrating drama is the loss of community in our schools and in society itself. If we want to rewrite the script to enable good schools to flourish, we need to rebuild community. Community building must become the heart of any school improvement effort."

— THOMAS SERGIOVANNI, *BUILDING COMMUNITY IN SCHOOLS*[46]

Thirty percent of all students entering ninth grade in public schools across the country will drop out of high school.[47] Half of Black and Hispanic students will not graduate.[48] Fifty percent of new teachers entering the schools will quit within the first five years of teaching.[49] Something is wrong with this picture. One can instinctively blame the students for failing to understand that their future depends on graduating with a solid educational foundation; blame their parents for not insisting that they stay in school; blame teachers for a lack of dedication. But we think Thomas Sergiovanni gets it right in the quote above. A distressing number of students and teachers don't feel they belong in their schools, don't see how what is asked of them fits into the kind of life they want to lead, and don't find the work of the school meaningful or relevant. Schools have to be places where students and teachers want to accept the challenges of teaching and learning and do the work because they see its purpose. And, they have to be places that are safe in both a physical and psychological sense, places where students can take the risks of learning and relating to others. Schools have to help students and teachers feel someone cares about them, is interested in what they have to offer to the school, and gives them a sense and reason to belong. Schools have to strive to be communities.

Democratic Communities

Sergiovanni sees community as the central experience that enables us to act democratically, with and for others in the common interest. He argues, "Democratic communities help students to be as well as to become. They help students meet their needs today as well as becoming tomorrow's caring and active citizens."[50]

Within each of our case study schools we found an understanding of and a desire to create these democratic communities and saw multiple ways in which arts programs contributed to that purpose.

The power of the arts to build community lies in what we described in previous chapters. When the arts are taken seriously by teachers, artists, and school administrators as works that make visible students' knowledge, insight, and experiences, learning begins to matter and a third space is created. Within this space, as we have seen, teachers and artists assist students to make connections between art works they are studying—a play by Shakespeare, a collage by Romare Bearden, an opera by Puccini—and their daily lives. Teachers encourage students to create original works that embody their personal insights and narratives. As teachers and other students respond to these works with respect and encouragement, a climate of openness and support is created, a space where the risks and rewards of learning are pursued and the fears of failure and embarrassment minimized. The classroom becomes a safe haven for revealing oneself and for developing capacities for interpersonal and intercultural understanding.

Sergiovanni writes that young people in schools have always had "subcultures"–large or small groups of students clustered around shared values, styles, and beliefs – and that there has traditionally been a "rift" between these subcultures and the cultures of the adults running schools. The "rift" is becoming a "chasm," he fears, and the "distancing not only makes [educator's] work difficult but places students at risk socially and behaviorally." For schools to be truly effective then, they must close this gap and adopt "strategies aimed at helping classrooms become democratic communities" that "can help students and adults come together to construct a standard for living in their schools together."[51] In this context, the ability of the arts to bridge students' and teachers' experiences is especially important.

As a teacher at Central Falls High School said, "In the arts, students become members of a community instead of subservient within it."

School as Community

The Grizzly Hill School is in a small community on the San Juan Ridge of the Sierra Nevada Mountains in northern California. When we visited the school early in our study, it had an enrollment of less than 100 students in kindergarten through eighth grade. It taught us a great deal about how schools can be transformed when school leaders consciously seek to create a sense of community within the school and beyond its walls, and the role that the arts may play in these processes.

Grizzly Hill describes itself as a "place-based school with a global perspective." There is an historic Native American presence in the region, though only nine Native American students attend the school. The large majority of students – eighty-four percent – are White. Three students are Asian and three Hispanic. Ninety-seven percent of the students fall below the poverty line. There could easily be a sense of isolation and limitation at Grizzly Hill often found in poor rural communities, as well as tensions among the population subgroups. The school made the intentional decision to expand the horizons of its students, first validating their experience of living on the ridge, the principal told us, and then "using it as a basis to explore the rest of the world." The arts, he said, were chosen as the means of achieving the two ends. The cultures, history, and ecology of the ridge are explored in integrated arts curricula, taught with the assistance of local artists. International artists also are brought to the school through grant money raised by the arts coordinator.

When we visited Grizzly Hill late in the school year, it was preparing to absorb the entire student body of the nearby Oak Tree School, which was being closed, as small rural schools often are, because of district budget constraints. Grizzly Hill itself had only 93 students and an influx of the new group of students could have disrupted the fabric of relationships in its student body. In response, the coordinator of arts at Grizzly Hill decided to bring Oak Tree and Grizzly Hill students together before the school year ended to collaborate in developing and presenting a joint dance and theatrical performance.

A theater artist partnering with the Grizzly Hill and Oak Tree schools on their joint production selected a book set in Bali, *Rice is Life*, by Rita Golden Gelman, as the basis of the production. The decision to focus on Bali was prompted by the opportunity to bring a traditional Balinese orchestra, Gamelan Sekar Jaya, to the ridge for a musical and dance performance. Orchestra members and dancers were invited to attend the production mounted by the students before later performing for the students and their families (see figure 34).

We arrived at the end of the final preparations and in time for the two performances. The students had studied *Rice is Life* and the history, culture, and climate of Bali. They had written and produced their play, titled *The Rice Fields of Bali: A Tribute to the People and Land of Bali*. Working with local dancers from the ridge community, students from Oak Tree had learned traditional Balinese dance movements and taken the roles of the characters in the play (see figure 35). Grizzly Hill students created masks for these characters, painted the scenery, designed the lighting, and handled the technical aspects of the show (see figure 36).

The two shows were intentionally not performed at the Grizzly Hill or Oak Tree schools but at the North Columbia School House Cultural Center

fig. 34 The Balinese dance company Gamelan Sekar Jaya
performs for Grizzly Hill students and families.

fig. 35 Grizzly Hill students give a performance based on traditional
Balinese costume and dance.

fig. 36 Grizzly Hill students paint sets for their Balinese performance.

nearby, where parents, teachers, and community members from both schools would come together to celebrate and symbolize their forging of a new community: a recognition and embrace of the ritual power of the arts.

After Gamelan Sekar Jaya attended the student performance, their lead dancer took a young student from Oak Tree aside to compliment her solo performance and to discuss Balinese dance technique and the meaning of the movements, a moment of recognition for the young dancer. The two dancers were featured on the cover of the next edition of the Grizzly Hill newsletter (see figure 37). The newsletter, which

BUILDING COMMUNITY

had previously been titled *Bear Facts: Grizzly Hill Update* now appeared as *The Ridge School Review: News from Grizzly Hill and Oak Tree Schools, Serving the Families of the San Juan Ridge.*

Connecting the School and the External Community

The efforts of Grizzly Hill's arts coordinator and other faculty members to build a sense of community for students reached beyond the school. The local community in which the school sits had historically held a negative view of the students at Grizzly Hill. To counter this image, the school made students' abilities visible in the community through visual artwork and performance.

fig. 37 An Oak Tree student poses with Gamelan Sekar Jaya's lead dancer.

The school placed student artwork in public spaces. For instance, student artwork was exhibited year-round at the local post office (see figure 38). These displays had high visibility because the post office is the one location on the ridge that virtually all residents visit, as is often the case in small rural communities without home mail delivery. The artworks made visible not only students' artistic talent but frequently expressed students' interests, reflections on life on the ridge, and their learning in subject areas such as science and social studies.

The postmaster who agreed to host the exhibits said, "Besides the wonderful talent that it's unbelievable the kids have, it's inspiring. Customers even make special trips in here, and it's wonderful to look at and it's just amazing, you know. People don't realize how talented the kids are until they come in here."

Students also take family members to the post office to show off their work. The postmaster said, "For the kids, it gives them a wonderful sense of pride because they're going, 'Oh Grandma, my picture's up there.' They know all the other kids and they'll say, 'That's Mary's picture, John's, and here's mine.' When grandparents are visiting from out of town, families make special trips, not even to buy stamps. Can I help you? 'No, we're just here to look at Mary's pictures,' because

fig. 38 Grizzly Hill student work hanging in the post office.

BUILDING COMMUNITY

they're excited and they're proud of them. So it's kind of like a postal art gallery — school postal art gallery."

The ability of the arts to build a community *around* a school was visible at other schools in our study. Central Falls High School students in the ArtsLiteracy and Human Creativity programs said the arts have helped them to counter the negative reputation the school had in the surrounding community. A Human Creativity student said, for example, that when they perform outside the school, "The reactions we get, they're like 'wow, I never thought you could do that.'"

An ArtsLiteracy teacher said the performances and exhibitions have "given everyone a very different perspective on the genius that is present within this school." As negative perceptions of the school are countered, he finds, there is potential for creating new sets of positive relationships and cohesion among students and faculty.

A teaching artist at Sheridan Global Arts and Communications School likewise told us of the importance of displaying student artwork widely in community settings. Not only is it important, she said, that "the kids learn what it's like to be an artist and to see their work up and exhibited," but it is important "to have the community looking at the artwork and realize that this is a great school, there are great kids there, a lot of good things are happening. It just breeds excitement."

Another teaching artist at Sheridan said that the school's partnership with local artists is "helping teachers, the parents, the kids know what's outside the walls; it's kind of expanding the classroom into the community."

In a rural area without many formal arts organizations, Clarkton School of Discovery has become an arts center for the wider community. "I think people in our community have seen performances at our school they would not normally see in our area," a teacher said. "Our parents are amazed at some of the drama performances we have had — that middle school students are able to perform at such a high quality" (see figure 39).

As was the case at Grizzly Hill, explicit efforts are made at other schools to use the arts programs as a way for students to develop a deeper understanding and appreciation of their local communities. Two assignments we observed at Newton D. Baker School of Arts asked students to study aspects of their communities and incorporate their findings into artwork. In one unit, fourth-grade visual art students studied the work of artist Maya Lin, in particular her Vietnam Memorial in Washington, DC, and her Civil Rights Memorial in Montgomery, Alabama. They also studied a memorial sculpture of Jesse Owens in Cleveland, Ohio, in order, their teacher told us, to help students understand why there are memorials and how they can help to recognize the important contributions that people make to their communities. The teacher wanted students to connect this study of the memorial form to their own lives, so she asked them to reflect on their communities and on who was special and important to them that they might want to honor. Students created memorials to these personal heroes, recognizing their contributions to their own lives or to the broader community. Student responses to this assignment served as a catalogue of community values and strengths (see figure 40).

fig. 39 Clarkton School of Discovery students perform *Alice in Wonderland.*

In another unit at Newton D. Baker, third-grade students examined the everyday lives of people in their community, selected a scene of interest to them, and captured it in a medium of their choice. The assignment was a response to a visual art standard from the Cleveland Municipal School District asking that students develop an understanding of *genre*—people engaging in everyday activities. Students depicted a range of scenes that invited viewers to see the community through their eyes (see figure 41).

In the Human Creativity program at Central Falls High School, engagement in the arts has helped students to change their attitudes toward the local community and to develop a sense of responsibility and a desire to contribute to community life. For instance, participants in Human Creativity and alumni of the program train with Human Creativity's director over summer breaks to learn how to teach the arts to other youth. Students and alumni now conduct after-school arts programs for elementary and middle school students in the district. One of the graduates said

fig. 40 Dr. Nebah, My Hero, plaster figure by Halie, Newton D. Baker School of Arts

fig. 41 Every Wednesday Things, drawing by Jennifer, Newton D. Baker School of Arts

that parents "love the program, because instead of being on the street and running around, students are doing something."

Human Creativity students want to start a community arts center to house arts programming year-round so others in the community can have the same arts experiences that they had in Human Creativity. One alumna said, "We want to open a building to start this program and extend it out into the community for kids and adults for every age group, to provide them with something to do, some type of activity for the teens other than just hanging out and stuff."

Interdependence and Creative Community

Students discussed the bonds that developed between them and the responsibility they began to feel toward one another in their arts activities. "I like the fact that I interact with a lot of new people in [Human Creativity] and we all—not really get close close—but we all become friends. It's like a small family. We go everywhere with each other and perform everywhere. It's awesome," a Central Falls high school student said.

"I was able to talk to different people and get different advice and get through my problems," another said. "It makes the people who are shy and don't really talk to anyone meet friends. This taught us a lot about real life." "Each person is needed here [in Human Creativity]," said still another.

"We stand up for each other and help each other out," a student in the Central Fall's ArtsLiteracy classes said. "We have to be there for the rest of the people." "We practice, everyone together," a classmate added. "And if there's something wrong, I will help you or someone else will." "If someone's absent, they could miss their part, we got to go with it. We got to work together to work everything out," another said. "We do understudies for all the parts."

Students in both programs told us that there had been times when they didn't feel like going to school and they had gotten a call from a teacher or another student reminding them that they had an important role they needed to play in their class. "I didn't want to let them down," one student told us, "because they needed me to do stuff for them. And then I like the play; *Romeo and Juliet* got me hooked. And I didn't want to let them down." Classmates called another student who had stayed home: "'You got to come to school,' they told me. I was, like, 'oh, all right,'" he said.

Several things are at play here. The students are not only motivated by friendship but by the requirements and demands of the artistic collaboration. The art form becomes the context within which they understand, negotiate, and accept their roles and responsibilities. The students are willing to do so because they have found personal meaning in the themes and narrative of the work—as the student put it: "*Romeo and Juliet* got me hooked"—and in helping to shape it into a collective expression to be presented to a public audience. The work, as we have discussed, matters and in its significance the students find the reason to master its technical requirements, its demand for discipline and persistence, to fulfill the obligations of their roles within the production.

These are the requirements of "active citizenship," the democratic behavior Sergiovanni urges be developed in schools. "[The] price," he writes, "is measured in obligations, duties, and commitment to the common good.... Democracy includes individual freedoms, but these freedoms can be guaranteed only by the strength of active citizenship."[52]

A Human Creativity alumna, describing the lessons she learned collaborating on dance performances, puts it another way: "You're a team. You're not just dancing by yourself; it's not a solo. It's a group."

A teaching artist in the program underlined the alumna's comment. He said that his student drummers who play for the dances are learning a similar kind of interdependence, an understanding that the dancers rely on them. He said the young drummers realized that the dancers had been struggling in the rehearsal because they had not been keeping the beat well, so the drummers increased their practice time in order to support their collaborators (see figures 42 and 43).

High school students were able to reflect upon and articulate their growth in these commitments. In the elementary and middle schools, teachers and parents commented on similar development that younger students revealed in their participation in an art form.

In the original opera programs at Newton D. Baker School of Arts and Peter Howell Elementary described earlier, for example, students engaged in what the educational researcher Dennie Palmer Wolf describes as "sustained and coherent collaboration." Students engaged in exchanges about how their individual contributions to their work would come together to realize their original opera. Teachers referred to this as learning teamwork, though perhaps a richer description is that students were developing the insights and skills to function as a creative community, embracing the different contributions of each into a story of real significance to them.

A teacher at Newton D. Baker talked in general about the effects of arts activities in the school: "[O]ver time everybody understands the rules [for making collaborative works]. Students participate more readily in a familiar structure; they become active participants and a supportive audience [for the works of other students]."

A third-grade teacher at Peter Howell said, "Students are expected to help each other in the arts classes. They take their [musical] instruments home and work with each other while they are away from

fig. 42 Central Falls High School dancers perform in *The Rhythm in Me.*

fig. 43 Central Falls High School drummers perform in *The Rhythm in Me.*

school. The helping carries over into other subjects. They are more willing to help each other in reading and math."

The director of the Lyric Theater in Tupelo which partners with Pierce Street Elementary School pointed to the demands and lessons of theatrical performance learned by young students: "You have to learn your lines and you've got to learn where you're supposed to be. Even the little bittiest [students] pick that up and the little knee biters get the sense of being where you're supposed to be when you're supposed to be there, and the notion of teamwork. You've got to make this stuff work because all of those folks are depending on you to be where you're supposed to be."

A movement teacher at Grizzly Hill said that in movement, his first- and second-grade students "start to explore what it's like to work with another person." As part of collaboration, the children learn, he said, to perform together, be an attentive audience for others, and teach one another, a set of basic social skills honed by the demands of the art form.

The band teacher at Sheridan captured well the impact of ensemble performance on developing both individual and social skills: "There is the group thing and you have all these individuals," she said, "and they're both valuable and they're both necessary. So you have to work with the individual and yet make the group work. That's an interesting process to make that happen, because they have to feel that they're there individually to do their own thing and they have to feel that they're part of this group to make a difference."

Empathy, Tolerance, and Imagination

Grizzly Hill teachers and administrators are explicit in their intention to use their arts programs to help students avoid or change negative perceptions of other groups or individuals, to use participation in arts activities as a path to empathy, tolerance, and the ability to grapple with moral dilemmas.[53]

"Reading skills won't define what is needed to succeed in the job market," said Grizzly Hill's principal. "Awareness of diverse cultures will be key. Textbooks don't provide this kind of information."

Grizzly Hill exemplified the powerful way in which the arts help students develop their capacity for empathy. There is a clear understanding among faculty and community members at the school that key to students learning to build understanding with others are their own experiences of revealing themselves – making themselves visible through their artwork and being understood and affirmed in their individuality by classmates and adults. These kinds of experiences in the arts engender a healthy sense of self and a willingness and capacity to affirm and appreciate the selves expressed by others.

Faculty and community members believe that these experiences can counter racial and ethnic stereotypes students may bring to the school, preparing students, for instance, for meaningful engagement with the local and international artists that visit the school. The school hosts many such visitors who present artistic programs expressive of their cultures. We met visiting Balinese artists at the school and heard about other guests from the Native American populations of the region and from West Africa.

A school board member at Grizzly Hill shared her opinion of the importance of these visits, "All of our schools up here in the mountains are White almost exclusively and as a result, we have kids who are prejudiced. They bring it from home. You don't hear about it too much unless they refer to something on TV or something like that. What some of the schools have done is they've tried to address it in a very direct kind of counseling approach. It doesn't work." The school arts coordinator, the board member said, "began bringing in all these cultural groups and getting the kids involved in these activities where they would learn things. None of it's presentation here; it's all participation. The kids around here had a concept of what Blacks are as opposed to Whites, also of what Africa is all about – a primitive country and all these kinds of things. They learned other things [from the performances], and with the Native American dance group as well. They learned how people function differently when the arts are an integral part of their lives. When you look at what's going on in the world right now, I think there is some real social value in that. It's hard to explain but I think the arts teach people to think intuitively about things rather than to think only in terms of how they are described. It gives people a chance to integrate what they feel into what they think and to absorb information differently and bring that back into their lives. That's how it works here." The arts, she said, provide new possibilities for seeing and thinking about the world.

At Dyett Academic Center High School, the setting is seemingly very different from Grizzly Hill. The student body is entirely African-American and the school is located in a major urban center, Chicago, yet students and teachers reported a similar need for experiences that help expand the horizons and understandings of the students.

One student explained, "A lot of kids only are exposed to certain things or just being around Black people. When you go out to the workforce, you're not going to be working only with Black people; you're going to be working with all cultures. So, you need someone there to learn different things and learn how to behave around different people. Diversity is important."

An artist teaching poetry and spoken word at the school said that was one of her goals. "My classes encompass a lot," she said. "I try to give them a different world outlook, and a broader world outlook than what they see in their neighborhoods or even on the news or even when they venture downtown or to the north side or something outside of their neighborhood.... I hope they pick up on that, but always bringing it back home and making it relevant to what they're going through."

The director of the Lyric Theater in Tupelo, Mississippi, summarized succinctly his belief about how the arts change the lives of young people in the ways espoused at Grizzly Hill and Dyett. "The key value of any variety of art in my judgment," he said, "is to open your mind to possibilities."

Opening the mind to possibilities is an act of the imagination, the ability to reach beyond one's own experiences, as Maxine Greene writes, to "feel one's way into another's vantage point," to see that things and people can be different than you first perceive them.[54] It is an essential component of empathy, an important capacity for building interpersonal and intercultural understanding.

As a student at Sheridan Global Arts and Communications School told us, "It feels good to have people admire your work." When people learn about you through your artwork, "then they'll be your friend."

We heard a similar sentiment at Central Falls High School. A student in the ArtsLiteracy program told us, "[When you're performing] you just feel like you're whole, like everyone knows you." An alumna of Human Creativity said that now that she is "out in the real world," she is building on her experiences in Human Creativity to better understand and deal with the complexities of life. "You can see different perspectives," she said. "[The Human Creativity program] gets you open-minded. It makes you a better person. It gives you a much better perspective on life. I really owe it to that program, I do, because not that I became popular, nothing like that, but, everyone [during her school days] is like, oh, she's the one that's always on stage, the 'one who dances.'"

Human Creativity participants are conscious that through their arts collaborations they have created an inclusive community that respects differences. "You don't go out and say 'this person's that,'" another alumna told us. "No. You don't know what that person is. Everyone dresses different, acts different, and everyone's attitude is completely different. We don't try to be like one another because we feel we can expose ourselves and show who we are. We don't have to be like that person, but we are still accepting." She added, "We started learning things about the arts. That helps, like you know, be part of a community. It kind of cut down stereotypes. We get to learn about other people's cultures." This was important in a school as racially and ethnically diverse as Central Falls, she told us. "We *look* like a piece of art," she said.

The principal at P.S. 130 in Brooklyn, New York, described her student population as "international." Many are recent immigrants or first generation Americans. There are seventeen languages spoken in the school. Her vision was to create a "peace school" where positive relationships among groups were fostered through processes that honor each individual and culture. Echoing the voices of teachers at Grizzly Hill and students at Central Falls, she found that the arts were a way in which subgroups could "make themselves visible and understood."

The principal told of one arts integrated unit that was done in collaboration with their partner organization, ArtsConnection. The class was studying Egypt and making mosaic tiles as part of that unit of study. She explained, "We are so diverse, and we had two children who did not want to sit together initially, whose parents were feuding and had horrible things to say about each other at home and the students were forced now to work on these tiles; they had to come up with a design, lay it down, very tedious work, and after the work was done and the children reflected on the piece, one of the kids was able to say something really deep like he initially did not want to do the work with his classmate, because they're very angry with each other and they'd been fighting and they'd done a lot of terrible things to each other, but they realized that they could still create something very beautiful together."

At P.S. 130 where more than a third of the students are immigrants from a range of different countries, opportunities such as these were important in allowing students to collaborate with each other to find meaning, even beauty, together. The principal said that there had been increasing urgency to build positive relationships among students, "We have a lot of children from Iraq, Iran, a lot of the countries that are in turmoil right now, Afghanistan. We've got tons of children from there, and so after September 11th, it was really very difficult for the other students to work through what was happening right outside our window. It was very hard for teachers to work through this horrific experience. And I think that when you put language aside, and you just use the common language of the arts, people are able to express themselves. Art gives them an opportunity to be able to talk without saying anything that's going to be lost in words."

"Kids need non-threatening ways of being able to work together and to see each other doing really hard work, but in ways that are not intimidating and in ways that say we can work together," the principal continued. "We can do this, we can create something fabulous, we can have a good time, we can have fun, without words interfering or creating misunderstandings."

She told of another unit that she felt illustrated the point. An artist was collaborating with a third-grade teacher on a unit integrating social studies and storytelling. The artist was helping students to understand, retell, and act out African folktales. "I structure my residencies on expression," the artist had explained. "So I always take a look at three different forms of expression: voice expression, body expression, and facial expression."

The teacher who worked with this artist told the principal that through the expressive and collaborative activities "a number of kids have now forged relationships." Acting out the stories using the artist's second two forms of expression (body and face), the principal said, allowed students to communicate in non-verbal ways.

"Now the kids are able to see how really good at pantomime and at improvisation some of their classmates are, who they otherwise totally ignored the whole year because [the classmates] really were very shy and unable to express themselves. So now they're willing to forge these relationships because they see there's something special about someone they hadn't noticed before. That's happening in the classroom," she said.

The educational researcher Rosario Carillo writes: "Working toward third space is useful because it is respectful and responsive to the cultural and linguistic diversity of learners. It is also a useful approach in understanding how to effectively support learners to negotiate a multiplicity of discourses as opposed to simply transmitting to them an official standard body of knowledge that is monolithic and monocultural."[55]

Third space allows students to define for themselves, and in dialogue with others, their own complex identity. Students of the same race or ethnicity may conceive of their identity – and the role of race and ethnicity in shaping that identity – differently, depending on the contexts in which they live and the interaction of the multiple dimensions of their lives including gender, language, neighborhood, and socio-economic and educational background. The third space opened by the arts provided an opportunity for students to engage and express these complexities outside of predetermined categories. These opportunities for developing a strong self-identity are important for students' individual development and important for their capacity to become part of a community.

As one of P.S. 130's partners at ArtsConnection told us, "art is about discovery – self discovery and discovery of others you are working with. This [discovery] causes the dynamic of the classrooms to change."

Community as a Foundation for Art and Learning

A teaching artist from P.S. 130 said that a sense of community is not only a byproduct of a meaningful arts learning experience, but may be a necessary condition for one to occur. "An audience can either hold you back or really push you forward," she said. "And my job as the arts educator is to provide as protective an environment as possible so that when you're out there risking it on whatever level, you are going to be safe and it is going to be okay."

Teachers and artists working in the ArtsLiteracy program at Central Falls High School shared this sentiment. Community building is the first step in the program's performance cycle. The staff of the Education Department at Brown University who designed the ArtsLiteracy Project notes that the relationship between the arts and community building is mutually reinforcing. Good arts practice demands a strong community in which it can take place, they believe, and strong arts practice helps to build community. They chose the dramatic arts as a central component of their program for their potential to foster community in classrooms. Through their inherently collaborative nature, these arts create a shared purpose and sense of belonging among students and teachers, and a medium for safe risk-taking.

As the ArtsLiteracy director told us, "Building community is one of the most important aspects of education."

A Central Falls High School teacher who partners with ArtsLiteracy told us that his goal is to build trust and create an environment for students to take the risks inherent in the dramatizations that are part of the learning method in the class. "The trusting relationships we establish are the foundation and the basis of all the learning that goes on in the class," he said. It typically takes a month to six weeks each year to fully involve the students in the processes used in the classes "to take the kinds of risks that are required to put yourself out there," he added.

He also offered advice to other educators for developing programs in schools with similar demographics. "Start with community building," he said. "Whether it's a literacy program or Algebra II; the critical nature of engaging students is creating that community."

Parents in the School Community

Parent involvement in schools is an important factor in student achievement and in the overall success and health of a school itself. But, getting and keeping parents involved can be difficult. Urban and rural schools similar to those in our study face a number of obstacles in engaging parents. Models of parent involvement that have emerged as the most successful across the country call for a more active role of the parent within the school: supporting teachers in classrooms, acting as coordinators of school activities, and serving on school planning and management committees. Families, however, can be stressed by economic pressures, which have ramifications for the amount of time they can spend at school and their ability to participate in the activities and committees many schools use as staples of parent involvement. School processes also often fail to bridge social and cultural divides that can alienate parents from schools. Schools need to offer parents experiences they find helpful, relevant, and rewarding for themselves and their children.

Across all ten case study schools, parents, teachers, and administrators reported that arts programs are one of the most successful means for offering parents these experiences. Administrators and teachers told us that parents are initially attracted to the school arts activities by an opportunity to see their students perform or exhibit their work. These opportunities allow for schools and parents to connect in a meaningful way, a departure point for parents to develop a greater sense of comfort and belonging at the school.

"When we have PTA meetings, we may have ten parents show up," a teacher at Pierce Street Elementary in Tupelo told us. "But when we have an arts festival, these halls are full because the parents get to see what their child has been doing. I think we're making small steps in getting our parents involved."

Pierce Street also provides arts experiences for parents as a means of engaging them when they come to the school. The arts coordinator said, "It's interesting to the parents if we use music or art or drama to engage them because just lecturing to parents [doesn't work]. To actively engage someone, you have to maintain their interest. I think it almost relieves their intimidation and just puts everyone at ease. It's a very effective tool for bringing parents into the school."

Clarkton School of Discovery in North Carolina holds its Parent, Teacher, Student Association (PTSA) meetings just before or after student performances to encourage a spillover into PTSA activities of parents attending the performances.

A parent who volunteers at Peter Howell Elementary in Tucson said, "It was like pulling out teeth to get parents here. But when you send a notice home and say, okay, your child's going to perform in this, and there are things going on in the individual classrooms, the parents would come for that." "And so we have lots of performances," the school principal added, "and I have seen parents who have taken buses and taxis. I've had parents who have gone to any extreme that they had to go because a lot of our parents don't have cars."

Teachers at Sheridan Global Arts and Communications School reported similar findings, telling us that since the school became arts-centered, parents feel more welcome and comfortable in the school, and that this comfort is responsible for greater parent involvement in all activities. "I've seen changes in how many parents come to parent-teacher conferences," a teacher said. "We've seen huge increases in the number of parents that come to school functions—like performances, family night, or curriculum nights."

At P.S. 130 in Brooklyn, a staff member from its arts partner, ArtsConnection, said they try to find non-threatening venues to make parents comfortable on school grounds. Their most successful events are family arts workshops held on several Saturdays during the school year. "We do a lot of our family art days out in the schoolyard," she said, "and neighbors walking by stop. They come over, they talk. People are starting to send their children to the school and it's becoming a real community school. [The principal] has worked very hard. She had a vision of how to involve the community. I think, when she saw, at the first family day with the arts that the arts presented a very non-threatening entry level, she realized that that was the way to go. And it's true. We had [an ArtsConnection artist] who was doing puppetry and storytelling. She did a Saturday afternoon workshop and we expected about fifty parents, which is a lot, and there were hundreds." At that time, students were working with this puppetry artist in arts integrated units in their classrooms (see figure 44). They were able to show their parents what they were learning. "The kids were showing their parents how to make shadow puppets and then they all got to stand in front of the screen and show the puppets to their parents, and it was just a wonderful experience," said the ArtsConnection staff member.

Other schools with large constituencies of parents who are not fluent in English similarly cited greater parent involvement as an important

fig. 44 A P.S. 130 student directs his shadow puppet performance.

effect of their arts programs. The arts provided nonverbal means of communications through which the parents could engage with the schools. The arts programs also brought parents and teachers together in a shared role, the role of audience for student work. A teacher at Peter Howell Elementary School said, "The parents who don't speak English or little English show up more and in greater numbers. They like to see their kids perform and after they get here, we can talk about their kids and what is happening in other programs of the school."

The principal at P.S. 130 told of one of her favorite stories about a family art day, at which a teaching artist was providing instruction in Chinese calligraphy. A P.S. 130 student and her grandmother, both Chinese, were attending the class. The grandmother, who did not speak English, watched as the teacher taught calligraphy but was incorrectly shaping one of the characters. The principal said that the grandmother mustered her courage, walked to the front of the room, took the brush out of the teacher's hand, and wrote the character correctly for the other participants to see. It was a transforming moment for the grandmother, the principal said. She had not felt comfortable in the school before, blocked in part by her lack of English. Able to contribute her knowledge and skill, share her traditions and culture, and to do so nonverbally through her art, she found a new level of comfort – assumed the important role of a teacher – in a place that had previously felt alien.

The principal told us, "She was welcomed into the building. It was like that experience made her part of the community. It was sort of like we were able to accept her on her terms because she had contributed what she knew best. I love that story. I think that's what happens with our kids, too. Once we're able to figure out how they can contribute and they do, that's it."

She added, "You become part of the community; the community will help you with all the things you don't know."

Perhaps that is the single most compelling message that we found in the schools we studied for this book. The arts create a third space in schools that is a place within which young people and adults are creative and vital, are liberated from barriers self-imposed or imposed by others, from the disconnections between their daily lives and the roles they assume in schools, from the fear of failure. It is a space in which students and teachers succeed and do so together as learners, as an open and inclusive community with a fulfilling and meaningful present and a hopeful future—the type of community that can be the foundation of a democracy, fulfilling the primary purpose of American public schools. ∎

Endings

I know you are about to close this book
But I guarantee if you take a look
You'll reflect
A thing or two, here or there
I know you've seen
Perspectives from many things
Sun and Moon, Dog and Cat, Ground and Sky
So, maybe we've sparked some inspiration
You now have our invitation
To take a look around you
There are opposites everywhere

fig. 45 Endings, poem by Carly; collage by Madeline, Peter Howell Elementary School

School Demographics[i]

SCHOOL NAME LOCATION	GRADES	TOTAL ENROLLMENT	% AMERICAN INDIAN, ALASKAN	% ASIAN	% BLACK	% HISPANIC	% WHITE	% FREE AND REDUCED PRICE LUNCH
Central Falls High School Central Falls, RI	9-12	794	0.4%	0.5%	10%	57%	32%	98%
Clarkton School of Discovery Clarkton, NC	6-8	358	0.8%	0.3%	38%	1%	60%	57%
Dyett Academic Center High School Chicago, IL	9-12	453	0%	0%	100%	0%	0%	62%
Grizzly Hill School North San Juan, CA	K-8	93	9.7%	3.2%	0%	3%	84%	97%
Hand Middle School Columbia, SC	6-8	943	0.1%	0.7%	49%	2%	48%	55%
Peter Howell Elementary School Tucson, AZ	K-5	407	2.7%	2.2%	5.6%	49%	38%	80%
Newton D. Baker School of Arts Cleveland, OH	K-5	608	0.3%	0.3%	73%	5%	22%	86%
Pierce Street Elementary School Tupelo, MS	K-3	477	0.2%	1.3%	56%	2%	41%	60%
P.S. 130 Brooklyn, NY	PK-5	649	0.2%	23.1%	22%	32%	22%	84%
Sheridan Global Arts and Communications School Minneapolis, MN	K-8	714	3.4%	31.5%	30%	3%	32%	67%

i   All figures were collected from Common Core of Data (CCD). CCD is a program of the U.S. Department of Education's National Center for Education Statistics and is a comprehensive, annual, national statistical database of information concerning all public elementary and secondary schools.

School Profiles

The descriptions that follow acquaint the reader with the basic facts about each of the ten schools discussed in *Third Space*: the demography and location of the school, the decisions that made the arts its central focus, and the types of arts programs provided to students. The information was gathered before and during our visits to the schools, which were completed in spring and fall 2002, and was subsequently verified by the schools. Changes no doubt have occurred since we visited: principals may have moved on, teachers retired or been reassigned, programs revised. For readers seeking current information, we provide the address and phone number of the school.

Central Falls High School

24 SUMMER STREET
CENTRAL FALLS, RI 02863
PHONE: (401) 727-7710

School Basics

Central Falls High School is an inner-city school in the heart of Central Falls, Rhode Island, located just outside Providence, the state capital. Central Falls is a city of one square mile with one of the state's highest concentrations of young people living in economically disadvantaged circumstances. Ninety-eight percent of Central Falls High School's 794 students are eligible for free or reduced-price lunch.

Many of the high school students are newly arrived in the United States from Central and South America, from the Cape Verde Islands, and from several Caribbean nations. Fifty-seven percent of the students are Hispanic, thirty-two percent White, ten percent Black, and one percent Asian/Pacific Islander or Native American. Twenty percent of the students arrive with few or no skills in the English language. Twenty-two percent of the students are enrolled in special education. The students, particularly those who are recent immigrants to the United States, are highly transitory. In a given year, forty percent of the student population will turn over between the beginning and end of the school year. The dropout rate at Central Falls High School is currently fifty percent, an improvement from eighty percent several years ago.

The Central Falls School District has had a difficult time in recent years meeting standards set by the state of Rhode Island, which has assumed an oversight role in the district and monitors its policies, programs, and academic performance, particularly in reading and mathematics.

Adopting an Arts Focus

Central Falls High School delivers arts instruction in discrete and integrated arts classes. The school's discrete arts offerings have been growing over the past fifteen years. Students can now take sequential classes in visual and performance art, which incorporates dance and theater, taking more advanced classes as they progress through high school. Students can also participate in a choral arts program. A visual art teacher offers classes in ceramics and jewelry; a choral director offers classes in choral music; a third teacher offers classes in studio art, photography, portfolio, and performance art. This last teacher founded and directs a program that clusters her art, photography, and performance art classes into a program called Human Creativity that now extends into after school multi-arts activities through funding from the federal 21st Century Community Learning Centers program. Human Creativity and an integrated arts program called ArtsLiteracy, introduced into the school in 1997 by Brown University in Providence, were the focus of the study reported in *Third Space*. Brown University's Education Department created the ArtsLiteracy program drawing on its research into the conditions and methods that best develop adolescent literacy. It is an integrated arts program based on the theory that adolescent literacy is promoted in communities of students actively engaged in arts experiences involving literature and theater, taught by teachers and professional artists working in collaboration.

The ArtsLiteracy program at Central Falls began to take root when one teacher of English as a second language participated in an early ArtsLiteracy summer training program Brown University conducts for teachers and artists. By June 1997, several English teachers, teachers of English as a second language, special education teachers, and history teachers had joined their colleague in becoming involved in ArtsLiteracy. About fifteen teachers in the building now implement the program in their classrooms.

Arts Programs in the School

Through ArtsLiteracy, teachers collaborate with actors, directors, photographers, and dancers from Rhode Island's arts community to devise and implement teaching plans based on a performance cycle that involves a close analysis of literary texts, dramatic enactment, writing, and original performances. Each unit of study is taught through a fifteen-session collaboration between teachers and artists. A mentor teacher is assigned to each team to help teachers and artists reflect on their practice as they engage in the performance cycle processes.

Student leaders from ArtsLiteracy provide professional development to teachers and artists who are beginning to participate in the program. These student leaders also serve as ambassadors for the program, presenting the work that they do in the program to local and national meetings of educators and policy makers.

Students in Central Falls' Human Creativity program receive their primary arts instruction from the program's founder and director, who teaches the visual and performance art classes at the school and also directs the after-school multi-arts program. Local artists conduct residencies in the program and help students develop skills in such areas as West African drumming, film, Latin dance, and theater. Alumni from the Human Creativity program also are part of the faculty. Under guidance of this team of teachers, the students each year mount two major, original, multi-art form productions, which they write, stage, and choreograph themselves. In addition, Human Creativity's students end each year with an exhibition of their visual art work as well as a showcase of their choreography and build toward a capstone class their senior year in which they can develop portfolios to be used in the college admissions process.

Students in the Human Creativity program are also leaders who not only help to direct the work of the program but who also work to garner support for it in the broader community, performing and speaking in front of district- and state-level policy makers and the general public, and providing professional development to teachers and artists. The students also teach arts in the elementary schools in their district to ensure that younger students have the same opportunities in the arts that they were granted.

Clarkton School of Discovery

NORTH COLLEGE STREET
CLARKTON, NC 28433
PHONE: (910) 647-6531

School Basics

Clarkton School of Discovery in Bladen County, North Carolina, is a magnet school enrolling students in grades six through eight. The town of Clarkton is rural with a population of approximately 740. Students who live in Clarkton's attendance zone are automatically granted admittance to the school, while those living in other areas must apply for admission, which is determined by a computerized lottery rather than performance measures, auditions, or entrance exams. Because Clarkton serves its surrounding community and is a magnet school for young people in other communities, its population is highly diverse and includes students from a variety of socio-economic and ethnic backgrounds. About 358 students attend Clarkton, and of those, sixty percent are White, thirty-eight percent Black, and the remaining two percent Native

American, Asian/Pacific Islander, or Hispanic. Fifty-seven percent of students at Clarkton are eligible for free or reduced-price lunch.

Adopting an Arts Focus

The town of Clarkton had been home to Clarkton Junior-Senior High School, which served grades six through twelve, but by 1993 the B'   school District closed the high school because the town was simply too small   ide enough students. That year a group of teachers and community members formed a task force to save the remaining school; its enrollment had fallen to only 149 students. The task force decided that creating an arts-based magnet school would resurrect Clarkton because it would allow them to serve students beyond the town limits. The task force developed a vision for a "School of Discovery," a middle level magnet school for grades six to eight with a mission to help "students discover their talents." The task force worked with the county board of education to develop a plan to keep the school open. A slate of diverse elective courses was at the heart of the school's effort to help its students find their individual talents. Teachers drew on their own interests to develop courses based on the North Carolina Standard Course of Study. These courses engage students in multiple ways and teach to different kinds of learning styles. Arts integration began to happen almost instinctually as a way to fulfill the school's new student-centered vision. The new school was officially named the Clarkton School of Discovery in 1994.

Clarkton saw an opportunity for external support and in 1996 joined the network of "A+ Schools," a program developed and supported by the Thomas A. Kenan Institute for the Arts. The program helps schools throughout North Carolina use the arts as a strategy to improve the performance of the whole school and not just specific curricular areas. Through the A+ network, the entire Clarkton faculty participated in professional development workshops and meetings to increase the sophistication and scope of their arts integration programs.

Reinvention of Clarkton got another boost in 1998 from a million dollar, three-year grant from the U.S. Department of Education's Magnet School's Assistance Program. This money was used primarily to add arts teachers to the school faculty and to purchase arts and technology equipment and supplies. When the grant expired, faculty and administrators had to find creative ways to keep the arts specialists in the school. The school's dance teacher became certified in language arts and their visual arts teacher in science. They each split their teaching time between two disciplines. Funding for the drama, video, and music specialist positions were partially cut. A classroom teacher trained herself in the use of the video equipment to keep the video electives alive, and another teacher similarly trained herself in the use of the school's music keyboarding lab. The drama and video programs also were revived in 2004 and 2005 by a nine-week artist-in-residence grant from the North Carolina Arts Council.

Arts Programs at the School

The school day at Clarkton is divided into seven approximately fifty-minute periods. The first four are dedicated to instruction in mathematics, communication skills, science, and social studies. Students participate in these classes grouped by grade level. As is the case in all North Carolina A+ Schools, arts integration and hands-on learning are used as instructional strategies in these non-arts academic classes.

The three afternoon classes are dedicated to electives. Students participate in three elective courses each quarter, unless they are taking a semester or year-round elective. Each elective course has been designed by a faculty member, often to support the content and goals of the morning courses. Arts electives include, but are not limited to, band, dance, drama, piano keyboarding, web-design, studio arts, and video. Many electives also focus on integrating non-arts academic subject content with the arts. Teachers draw on their strengths to design these classes and on the support from the schools' arts specialists.

Integrated arts electives include Scientific Illustration, which combines science and the visuals arts; Math in a Basket, in which students study the connections between math and art; Art Down Through the Ages, which integrates the arts with social studies; and My Roots, My Life, and My Dreams, a class combining communications skills and multiple art forms.

Dyett Academic Center

555 E. 51ST ST
CHICAGO, IL 60615
PHONE: (773) 535-1825

School Basics

Dyett Academic Center is in the historic Washington Park neighborhood on the south side of Chicago, on the border of the 1,000-acre park of the same name. Once one of the city's premier addresses, it was home to a burgeoning community of African-American-owned theaters, restaurants, and stores. Subsequently, the neighborhood went into a period of decline as the Robert Taylor Homes – the largest public housing development in the nation – and many of the surrounding properties fell to neglect or demolition. The public housing development itself has dwindled to only two buildings, and single-family homes as well as condominium properties are sprouting up on previously vacant lots in the areas surrounding Dyett Academic Center and Washington Park. Dyett opened in 1972 and until 1998 served only students in grades six through eight. High school grades were added recently with a first class graduating in 2003. The school now enrolls 632 students in grades seven through twelve; 453 are in the high school which was the focus of our study at Dyett. All of the students are African-American. Dyett suffers much the same as other urban schools with high student turnover in a transitioning neighborhood. Its truancy rate is twenty-nine percent and attendance rate is eighty percent, both contrasting to statewide figures of two percent and ninety-four percent respectively. It has a seventeen percent dropout rate. Sixty-two percent of the students are eligible for free or reduced-price lunch.

Adopting an Arts Focus

Dyett is conveniently located near public transportation, with direct routes to Columbia College Chicago, one of the city's premier arts institutions. Columbia College has been instrumental in developing arts programs and experiences for students and teachers at Dyett.

The college's primary relationship with the high school is coordinated by the college's Center for Community Arts Partnerships through what is known as GEAR UP, a national initiative aimed at increasing college enrollment and retention of student populations underrepresented in higher education. GEAR UP is an acronym for Gaining Early Awareness and Readiness for Undergraduate Programs.

Columbia's GEAR UP program with Dyett includes year-round in-school services, after-school services, and summer services. Columbia faculty and upper-level college students work with Dyett teachers to provide integrated arts programs during the school day, as well as in the after-school programs. The Columbia staff arranges experiences on the college campus in the form of tours of the academic departments, classroom visits, and events that showcase collaborative works created by the students and faculty of the college and Dyett. Dyett students also enroll in the college's high school summer institute where they can earn up to three, transferable credit hours in college level classes.

Columbia's involvement brings new expertise in the visual and performing arts, literature, and technology to Dyett students and faculty, and also expands the range of arts available to the students at the school, such as pottery, photography, African and modern dance, graphic illustration, and film. At the same time, students learn that the arts can be a profession as well as a vehicle for self-expression and for developing intellectual skills that will support lifelong learning.

Arts Programs at the School

In executing arts-integration projects, classroom teachers are paired with artists from Columbia College Chicago faculty and staff, as well as with local artists from other community-based organizations, including academic and cultural institutions in the Hyde Park/University of Chicago neighborhood near the school. To garner acceptance from Dyett teachers, staff from the college's Center for Community Arts Partnerships solicited participation from teachers of all academic subjects at the high school grade levels through surveys and a series of meetings between project personnel and Dyett staff members. Dyett teachers suggested specific projects for their students that tied into their class curricula. The teachers also identified the specific skills they themselves would bring to program planning and implementation. Initially, arts programming only occurred during school hours. However, as more students and teachers began to see the benefit of teacher-artist partnerships, sessions were extended to after school. Teachers, who prior to their involvement could not find a way to fit art into their days, became advocates for the program, integrating the arts into an array of subjects at the school. Dyett English teachers worked with a local poet and a fiction writing instructor from Columbia to produce an anthology of student work. Maggie Brown, daughter of legendary jazz musician Oscar Brown, Jr., worked with a core of students to form a vocal ensemble. In a comic strip class students produced a comic book of their own under the instruction of a Dyett teacher who, as a practicing artist, has produced his own comic book series. One student from the school also published his own comic as a result of this experience.

Columbia, through the GEAR UP program, has involved a range of departments at the college in collaboration with Dyett, including the English and the fiction writing departments, the science institute, and the radio department. Activities on the campus were expanded and strengthened as Dyett students began to request different types of programs and take on leadership roles in creating projects that were of interest to them. The campus experiences address the larger purpose of GEAR UP, which is to motivate and prepare students to go on to higher education. From Dyett's first graduating class of 2003, three students enrolled at Columbia itself.

Grizzly Hill School

P.O. BOX 529
NORTH SAN JUAN, CA 95959
(530) 265-9052

School Basics

Grizzly Hill is a kindergarten through grade eight school serving a rural community on the San Juan Ridge of California in the densely forested foothills of the Sierra Nevada Mountains. Of the school's 93 students, eighty-four percent are White and nearly ten percent are Native American. Ninety-seven percent of the students are eligible for free and reduced-price lunch. Due to the high percentage of eligible students, the school provides free breakfast and lunch to all students every day. The closest community to Grizzly Hill is the small town of North San Juan, which is nine miles away. Many Grizzly Hill families live on privately maintained dirt roads that wind far beyond the reaches of electric power lines or access to public transportation.

Adopting an Arts Focus

Certified, part-time music and visual arts teachers provided the students at Grizzly Hill with arts instruction until severe funding cuts in the mid-90s led to the elimination of these positions and almost ended arts education at the school. However, the arts remained important to the staff, faculty, and community, and they found a new approach to arts education, one that extended beyond the walls of the school. They reached out to develop partnerships with musicians, painters, potters, poets, and other artists in the local community who came to the school to lead the students in a variety of arts projects. The entire school staff got involved, including the school's maintenance man, an accomplished musician, who helped the middle school students learn to play instruments and to form a rock and roll band. With funding support from the national Rural School and Community Trust, a support agency to rural schools initially funded by the Annenberg Foundation, the school hired an arts coordinator in 1997. The following year a specific classroom was designated an arts space and renamed the "Heart Room" to signify the central and important role of the arts in the school. The coordinator teaches visual and performing arts, assists classroom teachers with arts integration, and coordinates the school's partnerships with local and international artists and with local cultural institutions such as San Juan Ridge's North Columbia School House (a one room schoolhouse that has been converted into a cultural center). Students present performances to community audiences at the center and in other locations, and hang their visual artwork at a gallery in the post office and throughout the community. The result is a partnership in the arts that benefits both the school and the community.

Arts Programs in the School

Grizzly Hill's curriculum and pedagogy are guided by the school's mission to be a "place-based school with a global perspective." Faculty focus on teaching students about the surrounding area on the San Juan Ridge and use students' understanding of their environment, history, and heritage as a bridge to understanding the lives and culture of other people. The school staff believes the arts are central to this purpose as expressions of other cultures and as ways for students to investigate, understand, and express their own cultures and personal understandings.

Students study the animal- and plant-life on the ridge, as well as the heritage and history of the cultures that make up its population, including the Native American cultures. Teachers and students also experience international cultures through performances and programs involving visiting international artists. The school stresses with students that, though the visitors are from all parts of the globe, they share a common bond with the students as artists. Grizzly Hill sees the arts as a language that students can use to communicate with these guests as well as with their immediate community. The school has welcomed Tibetan Buddhist monks; Native American singers, dancers, and storytellers; Andean musicians; Congolese and Senegalese drummers; and other visual and performing artists. Grizzly Hill also strives to integrate a concern for the natural environment through all of its programs.

In addition to hanging their work in a gallery at the local post office, students have had paintings of birds adorn the walls of the California Department of Motor Vehicles, and they have created flags representing different types of bears and hung them at the North Columbia cultural center (a project modeled after Tibetan prayer flags and done to welcome a visiting group of Tibetan monks). Grizzly Hill believes the arts are not only a tool for learning but also ways students can be of service to the community and the world.

Hand Middle School

2600 WHEAT ST
COLUMBIA, SC 29205
PHONE: (803) 343-2947

School Basics

Hand Middle School in Columbia, South Carolina's state capital, is located in a middle and upper class, largely White, urban neighborhood but serves students in grades six through eight from several surrounding communities and has an ethnically and socio-economically diverse student body. Of the 943 students that attend Hand, forty-nine percent are Black, forty-eight percent White, and three percent Native American, Asian/Pacific Islander, or Hispanic. About half of the students are eligible for the free or reduced-price lunch program.

Adopting an Arts Focus

Hand has used the arts to generate a new image of the school. As recently as 1998, the school had not responded to the changing demographics and needs of its student population. Achievement was languishing below the 50th percentile on standardized test scores and the school was developing the reputation of having an uncontrollable school climate. It needed to be turned around. A new principal signaled with her first hire—a former policeman as disciplinarian—that safety in the school would be a major concern and steps would be taken to increase school attendance by countering apathy and instilling a sense of responsibility in students. Her next step was to analyze the faculty, and impressed with the arts teachers at the school, she concluded that their strengths could be built on to create an arts-centered school that would serve as common ground for the school's diverse student and community population. She asked a team of teachers, administrators, parents, and community members to write a grant to fund release time for the arts teachers to engage the school faculty in designing and implementing an integrated arts strategy. They called the effort the "Renaissance Project" and the design team became known as the "Renaissance Team." The principal and the team used three rationales for adopting an arts strategy: arts integration would be fun for students, it would distinguish Hand from other schools, and it could raise student test scores. The school also joined the Arts in the Basic Curriculum (ABC) network, a state-wide project of the South Carolina Arts Commission and the South Carolina State Department of Education that assists schools to become more arts focused by developing arts-integrated plans and programs.

Since making the decision to become an arts-based school, Hand has seen an eighty-five percent increase in the test scores of its African-American students. It has also been recognized by the South Carolina Department of Education in its Exemplary Writing Hall of Fame, by the U.S. Department of Education as a National Blue Ribbon School of Excellence, and in 2001 by *Time* magazine as a National School of the Year.

Arts Programs in the School

Eighty-five percent of Hand's students are enrolled in discrete fine and performing arts classes, and all students participate in integrated arts classes which have become a central part of the school's curriculum. There are three major components to the curriculum. The first consists of lessons that combine arts instruction with other subjects, such as math, science, and social studies. These integrated arts lessons are developed and taught by classroom teachers who have the freedom to design their own lesson plans.

The second component of the curriculum is thematic instruction that takes place with student teams. Students in each grade level are divided into two or three teams of 100 to 125 students. Students spend the entire school year in classes with their teams. The teachers of each team share a common planning period and at the beginning of the school year choose common themes to frame their curricula. The students then work with the same theme as they move from class to class. For example, students study weather patterns in science, write original poems and fiction about the weather in language arts class, and study the effects of weather on ancient structures in history.

The third component of the curriculum is also thematic, but rather than being team-based, it is school-wide. Every year, teachers are selected to be members of the Renaissance Team, the group of teachers, parents, and administrators that develops and oversees the school-wide theme. All instruction throughout Hand culminates in a day-long event in which each grade level creates and hosts an event for students in other grades. For example, a recent school-wide theme was *renaissance*. Eighth-grade students focused on the Harlem Renaissance and played the part of famous poets, while seventh-grade students focused on the Renaissance of ideas that took place in post-1940 America, and sixth graders hosted a medieval fair.

Newton D. Baker School of Arts

3690 W. 159TH ST
CLEVELAND, OH 44111
PHONE: (216) 252-2131

School Basics

Newton D. Baker School of Arts is a kindergarten through grade five arts magnet school with a lottery-based admission system on the west side of Cleveland, Ohio. The school serves 608 students. Seventy-three percent are Black, twenty-two percent White, five percent Hispanic, and one percent American Indian or Asian/Pacific Islander. Eighty-six percent of the students are eligible for a free or reduced-price lunch. Students come to the school from all sections of the Cleveland Municipal School District.

Adopting an Arts Focus

In 1993, a school principal in the Cleveland School District approached the newly appointed district superintendent and got permission to create an arts magnet school. The principal and a group of teachers had experience with Discipline Based Arts Education (DBAE), the art education model designed and promoted nationally by the Getty Education Institute for the Arts. The principal and teachers used the model to develop a plan to integrate, strengthen, and expand the arts into the curriculum and programs of the existing Newton D. Baker school.

In order to ensure that all faculty understood and embraced the DBAE art education philosophy and teaching techniques, all new staff were required to take discipline-based art education courses. The principal stressed that they would be working in a demanding environment and that the processes of getting an arts-centered curriculum off the ground would be challenging and time-intensive. Teachers in different grade levels met at least once a month to plan arts integrated lessons and to discuss strategies for helping students reach high levels of academic performance. Parents were invited to "open days" to observe the new programs to build their support for the new direction of the school. The school recruited teaching artists from the community to work with teachers and students to integrate arts into the academic curriculum and raised funds from corporations to buy art supplies and to pay the salaries of the artists-in-residence.

Arts Programs in the School

Arts integration is the heart of the curriculum at Newton D. Baker. Each year a theme is selected, focusing on an international region and its cultures, for example, Asia, Africa, Europe, or Latin America; or a region or culture within the United States, for example, Cleveland, Ohio, Native American culture and history, or African-American culture and history. The school staff meets for two days in August each year to discuss that year's theme, the goals of the integrated arts programs, and their plans and activities.

All the thematic and arts-integrated lessons and units address three essential questions, which have been developed over time by the staff: 1) How does this object, artwork, artifact, or performance tell about social ways of life (e.g., rituals, norms, behaviors, traditions, celebrations, customs)? 2) How does this object, artwork, artifact, or performance tell about social values and beliefs? and, 3) How does this object, artwork, artifact, or performance reflect how cultural groups change over time—past, present, and future?

Integrated units are taught by DBAE-trained classroom teachers independently or in partnership with the school's arts specialists or teaching artists from community arts partners, such as the Cleveland Museum of Art or the Cleveland Opera. The units culminate in a major event or performance at the end of the year.

In addition to integrated arts classes, all Newton D. Baker students participate in discrete arts classes in visual arts, dance, drama, and vocal and instrumental music. Teachers identify students to participate in advanced art electives (e.g., super choir or art club). These classes are scheduled as "pullouts" where students leave their regular classrooms to participate in these extra arts electives. In order to make this scheduling system work, students who are pulled out have "peer partners" in their classes who help them catch up on any missed work and keep extra folders of the relevant assignments. Students are responsible for keeping up to speed in all of their classes. No pullouts occur during mathematics and reading classes.

Family and community participation play important roles at Newton D. Baker. In order to ensure that families are involved in the creation of the curriculum, the school has created an arts curriculum committee that consists of a general classroom teacher from each grade level; a Title I-funded science and writing teacher; a visual arts teacher; the school's program coordinator, principal, and family liaison; and two parents.

Each year, parents host an arts festival at the beginning of the school year where they and their children complete an arts integrated unit together.

Peter Howell Elementary School

401 N. IRVING
TUCSON, AZ 85711
PHONE: (520) 232-7200

School Basics

Peter Howell Elementary School in the Tucson Unified School District in Arizona enrolls 407 students in kindergarten through grade five. Forty-nine percent of the students are Hispanic, thirty-eight percent White, six percent Black, three percent Native American, and two percent Asian/Pacific Islander. Half of the students are learning English as a second language. Peter Howell's student body is economically diverse. Many students come from the middle class neighborhood surrounding the school, but under a desegregation order about half of the students are bused to Peter Howell from other parts of the city, including more economically disadvantaged neighborhoods. Approximately eighty percent of Peter Howell's students are eligible for free or reduced-price lunch.

Adopting an Arts Focus

When a new principal walked into Peter Howell Elementary School in Tucson in 2000, she found teachers using whistles in an attempt to control noise and chaotic behavior among the students. She decided to replace the shrill with the soothing, installing speakers throughout the building to broadcast classical music during the day and hanging works of art on the walls: a series of statements that the aesthetics of the school could and should influence the learning and behavior of students. Her own background included music study and also graduate work that included review of the emerging research into the relationships between brain functions and the arts. She had also learned from her previous experience that the arts were avenues to learning for lower income students. A music teacher was hired immediately to integrate music into the curriculum.

The principal found common cause with the fine arts department of the Tucson Unified School District, which was developing a music-centered arts integrated curriculum called Opening Minds Through the Arts (OMA) based in part on these same premises about the connections between the arts and brain development, specifically identifying the connections between music learning and student intellectual development. Peter Howell became one of the pilot schools for the new curriculum.

Recent evaluations of the OMA program indicate that it has been successful at Peter Howell and at other schools in the district in improving student achievement, including increasing standardized test scores. The state of Arizona has announced it will seek to replicate the approach at schools across the state.

Arts Programs in the School

Peter Howell implements the OMA program school-wide and integrates the arts across the curriculum. Peter Howell employs a full-time music teacher and all students study the recorder and violin. Students also work with teaching artists who conduct residencies in the arts and in non-arts classes, again integrating arts instruction with the teaching of other academic subjects.

Peter Howell's kindergartners focus on auditory acuity and work with a string quartet or woodwind trio from the University of Arizona or the Tucson Symphony Orchestra. First-grade students work with University of Arizona opera students to enhance their language and writing abilities; they develop and perform original operas based on literary masterpieces. Students in the second grade work with dance specialists to interpret and respond to music while focusing on collaboration, critical thinking, and creative problem-solving. In the third grade, students learn how to compose original music to assist them in the development of decoding skills believed to be important for reading such as abstract reasoning skills and spatial intelligence, both being important for many disciplines including mathematics. Fourth-grade students further their decoding skills, abstract reasoning, and spatial intelligence, while those in the fifth grade use a thematic approach to compose, direct, stage, and perform original musical and musical theater productions. An after-school program called Project Shine, funded by the federal 21st Century Community Learning Centers program, offers a range of academic development programs, including high-quality instruction in the visual arts.

Pierce Street Elementary School

1008 PIERCE STREET
TUPELO, MS 38801
PHONE: (662) 841-8940

School Basics

Pierce Street Elementary School has the most diverse school population in the Tupelo School District in Mississippi, enrolling 477 students in kindergarten through third grade. Fifty-six percent of students are Black, forty-one percent White, and three percent Hispanic, Asian/Pacific Islander, or Native American. Pierce Street serves the largest percentage of English language learners and homeless students in the district. Sixty percent of the students qualify for free and reduced-price lunch. Federal housing officials and government consultants describe the school's population as virtually identical to inner city schools in major metropolitan areas in the United States.

Adopting an Arts Focus

Beginning in the 1994-95 school year, Pierce Street began a process of revitalizing teaching and learning through a deliberate infusion of the arts as discrete areas of study, and as an integrative focus for all subjects and areas of the curriculum. Based on its Early Prevention of School Failure assessment and other pre-testing data, the Pierce Street staff concluded that a large percentage of the school's students were entering kindergarten severely delayed in the areas of expressive and receptive language as well as motor, auditory, and visual skills. Pierce Street's teachers and administrators believed that the best way to address the diverse learning styles and rates of their students was to integrate arts into the school curriculum. All students would then have opportunities to make meaningful work, to better express themselves, and to be valued by others for their accomplishments.

Building on this inclusive philosophy and vision for the role of the arts at Pierce Street, the school in 1995-96 began participating in the Whole Schools Project of the Mississippi Arts Commission, a project designed to help schools implement school-wide, arts-centered reform strategies. At the beginning of the 1996-97 school year, Pierce Street began implementing the Whole Schools reform through overarching, interdisciplinary thematic strands as the basis of instruction in all grades. In preparation for the introduction of this thematic approach, teachers and arts specialists rethought the existing curriculum to ensure that the arts were integrated well across other academic disciplines, and that the arts and non-arts content would become mutually reinforcing. Pierce Street's arts initiative, titled "The Discovery Zone," has yielded high-quality arts experiences for students, staff, administrators, parents, and community members.

Staff development was a central component of the plan. The entire staff at Pierce Street was formally trained in the Discipline-Based Arts

Education approach of the J. Paul Getty Institute for Art Education and regularly participated in the Mississippi Arts Commission's Whole Schools Project institutes and retreats. Additionally, the entire Pierce Street staff engaged in monthly staff development with professional artists. In order to ensure that the arts integration at Pierce Street maintains its high standards and is constantly growing, new staff members beginning at Pierce Street are assigned mentors to assist them in implementing the Whole Schools Project.

Arts Programs in the School

Students at Pierce Street receive sixty minutes of instruction each week in music, movement/dance, media, and Spanish. Sixty minutes of drama and visual art instruction are offered in alternating weeks. Grade level teachers, arts specialists, and resource teachers plan their respective units together, discussing guidelines, strategies, expectations, and evaluations for each unit. Artist residencies provide Pierce Street students and staff an opportunity to use the arts as a tool for learning and to stay connected with the surrounding community. In an effort to ensure that teaching artists are competent in their discipline and capable of being effective teachers, the teaching artists are chosen from the roster of artists selected and trained by the Mississippi Arts Commission.

P.S. 130

70 OCEAN PARKWAY
BROOKLYN, NY 11218
PHONE: (718) 686-1940

School Basics

P.S. 130 Elementary School in Brooklyn, New York, enrolls 649 students in pre-kindergarten through fifth grade. Seventeen different languages are spoken by its students, reflecting the diversity of the Brooklyn community it serves. Twenty percent of the students are recent immigrants from Pakistan, Bangladesh, and Russia. Forty-four percent are English language learners. Eighty-four percent are eligible for free and reduced-priced lunch.

Adopting an Arts Focus

In 1989, P.S. 130 began a relationship with ArtsConnection, a private, nonprofit arts-in-education organization in New York City. The school initially participated in ArtsConnection's Young Talent Program, which provides students with talent or interest in music, dance, or theater up to forty hours of in-school and after-school training in their chosen area. Based on the success of the Young Talent Program, P.S. 130's principal expanded the partnership with ArtsConnection so all students could benefit from the arts experiences. Ongoing long-range planning was, and continues to be, the essential component of the partnership. A goal of a first three-year plan was to create a safe space for students to learn the English language by using the arts to develop trust and a sense of community in the school. A second three-year plan seeks to develop literacy skills through arts integration, focusing in particular on storytelling, puppetry, and performance. The partnership brings teaching artists into each classroom every year. Full-time visual arts and music specialists also provide instruction to students.

Arts Programs in the School

Since 1998, ArtsConnection and P.S. 130 have integrated sequential visual arts and music programs into the school's social studies curriculum. Beginning in 2001 the school also chose to focus on literacy and language skills because of its rapidly diversifying population and the high percentage of students learning English as a second language. To do so, the partners designed a sequential theater arts curriculum to develop speaking, listening, and writing skills and to deepen story comprehension. In 2001 they were able to implement this theater arts curriculum with support from an Arts Education Model Development and Dissemination Grant from the U.S. Department of Education. In kindergarten and first grade, students develop original stories and traditional tales through the integration of visual arts, creative movement, drama, and puppetry. Storytelling and creative dramatics are the focus in the second and third grade and students interpret and retell stories through vocal, physical, and emotional expression. Fourth and fifth graders learn the formal theater arts, studying the basic elements of acting and playmaking through collaborative activities.

The relationship between P.S. 130's classroom teachers and their artist colleagues is central to successfully integrating the arts into the curriculum. A school-wide policy requires its classroom teachers to meet with their artist partners regularly over the course of the semester. The classroom teacher and teaching artist partner to identify specific learning goals in social studies or language arts, agree upon the set of classroom activities that the artist will conduct and determine how the teacher can best support and participate in the instruction. Teachers and visiting artists hold meetings on a regular basis during the year to review and evaluate their goals, achievements, and progress. Students also engage in structured meetings led by the classroom teacher, teaching artists, or members of the ArtsConnection staff to reflect on and articulate what they have learned.

As part of their federal grant, ArtsConnection and P.S. 130 teachers and teaching artists are researching whether and how artist-teacher partnerships facilitate the students applying storytelling skills to learning and achievement in literacy and other subjects.

Sheridan Global Arts and Communications School

1201 UNIVERSITY AVE. N.E.
MINNEAPOLIS, MN 55413
PHONE: (612) 668-1130

School Basics

In 1990-91 Sheridan Elementary School was renamed Sheridan Global Arts and Communications School, the first step in becoming an arts magnet serving the northern half of Minneapolis, Minnesota, an economic empowerment zone. The student population in 2000 of 714 in kindergarten through grade eight was selected by lottery. Thirty percent of the students are Black, thirty-two percent Asian/Pacific Islander, thirty-two percent White, three percent Native American, and three percent Hispanic. Of the Asian student population, ninety-five percent are Hmong children born in the United States, especially to first-generation immigrant families, but who enter Sheridan testing at zero-level in English. Approximately seventy-five percent of all Sheridan students come into kindergarten with no book experience. Significant numbers of students in each grade are challenged by poverty, family instability, and lack of early childhood preparation. Sixty-seven percent of the students receive free or reduced-priced lunch.

Adopting an Arts Focus

In 1972, busing in Minneapolis began as a result of court-ordered school desegregation. When Black students were bused into Sheridan, many local parents transferred their children to private Catholic schools. These dramatic changes in the school demography contributed to years of instability. The school was closed from 1982 until 1988 during a period of district-wide enrollment decline. It reopened in 1988 for grades three to six. In 1989, a new principal was assigned to lead the school. When she arrived, she found that student achievement was low, the student body exhibited unusually high numbers of behavioral problems, and both student and teacher morale was poor. Teachers spoke despairingly about the changes in the Sheridan population, questioning whether such highly mobile students who lived in poverty could learn.

Minneapolis had created an arts magnet program in the late seventies on the Southside of the city, a program which was highly popular with parents. For years the school had not been able to accept all the students whose parents selected it as their school of choice. The district superintendent and the new principal at Sheridan agreed that a group of thirty-five parents who were unable to enroll their children in the Southside magnet that spring be asked to help introduce arts program at Sheridan. The principal believed strongly that the arts would be the best vehicle to improve the school's climate and performance.

She began by recruiting a kindergarten teacher from the Southside arts magnet to help her create an arts integrated kindergarten. The following year the school became part of a federal grant to assist Minneapolis in developing magnet programs in racially isolated schools. The vision for Sheridan then became a fine arts magnet school to serve students in kindergarten through grade eight. With the magnet grant, the principal was able to hire a teacher as arts coordinator. First, second, and third grades were added and also took on the arts-centered curriculum. In each succeeding year, the arts focus expanded as the grade levels grew until Sheridan became an arts integrated kindergarten through grade eight magnet in 1998-99.

Sheridan has found ways to continually strengthen and expand its arts programs. In 1995 the school received a federal grant to teach Hmong arts and culture to all Sheridan students, along with Hmong literacy to its Hmong families, who in turn worked with the school to teach their arts and culture. In 1997 an Annenberg Challenge grant was awarded to the school district and Sheridan became part of the ensuing Arts for Academic Achievement program, using its share of funds to support arts programs in the school. In 2001 the U.S. Department of Education awarded a Model Arts Education and Dissemination Grant to the district in partnership with the state arts agency, the Perpich Center for Arts Education. Sheridan's history and experience in the arts informed the design of the model. The U.S. Department of Education also awarded Sheridan a Comprehensive School Reform Grant in 2003, recognizing its arts-centered program as a school-wide reform model.

Arts Programs in the School

Sheridan's mission statement expresses how the values and goals of the school shape the curriculum: "The purpose of the Sheridan Global Arts and Communications School is to empower its students to grow and to work successfully in a world in which all countries are becoming more and more interdependent with each other. Students pursue a multi-cultural curriculum emphasizing communication and technology in the visual, performing and media arts."

The content and sequence of programs and courses reflect this multidisciplinary emphasis. While students in kindergarten through grade five study language arts, science, and mathematics at each level, they also are progressively exposed to the arts to develop artistic abilities and appreciation. In these early grades, they engage in an average of thirty-eight hours of class time per year in dance, visual art, vocal music, media arts, and foreign languages. Each first- through sixth-grade student also studies a stringed instrument; in fourth grade, students can choose to study a band instrument in addition to strings. Seventh- and eighth-grade years are more focused and each student concentrates on one of the following arts areas: band/orchestra, visual art, dance, media arts, vocal music, or technology. During these "focus years," students spend about 120 hours a year working in their arts area, and they have opportunities to continue learning French and to study African music. Along with the arts, multiculturalism is emphasized at Sheridan, both in curriculum and in school activities. Culturally themed dinners are held where students and their families enjoy African-American, European-American, and Hmong meals.

Collaboration is a key component of Sheridan's program. Arts specialists work closely with teachers of math, science, and language arts. The school also uses visiting artists who bring specific skills and areas of expertise to the program. The school's two fine arts coordinators are responsible for managing the communications and planning among in-school educators and teaching artists from the community.

About the
Arts Education Partnership

The **Arts Education Partnership** is a coalition of national, state, and local education, arts, government, and philanthropic organizations. The Partnership was founded in 1995 by the U.S. Department of Education and the National Endowment for the Arts in cooperation with the National Assembly of State Arts Agencies and the Council of Chief State School Officers, which is the national association of state education agencies. The Partnership commissions, conducts, and publishes research; identifies and promotes effective national, state, and local policies supportive of arts education; conducts forums and conferences on the role of the arts in responding to education issues and needs; and serves as a clearinghouse on resources that support arts education.

About the Authors

Richard J. Deasy has been the director of the Arts Education Partnership since its founding. He has led AEP's efforts to produce seminal reports and research studies that demonstrate the positive impact of the arts on students, schools, and communities and that provide guidance to policy makers and practitioners on how to create that impact. Most recently he commissioned and edited AEP's compendium of studies, *Critical Links: Learning in the Arts and Student Academic and Social Development.* Prior to assuming the leadership of AEP, Mr. Deasy has been a senior official in two state departments of education, responsible for the areas of curriculum, instruction, assessment, and legislative relations. He also served as chief executive of an international and cultural exchange organization, and was an award-winning journalist. Mr. Deasy has taught at the secondary and university levels.

Lauren M. Stevenson, as senior associate for research at the Arts Education Partnership, was principal investigator for the research project culminating in *Third Space*. She also served as assistant editor of the AEP compendium, *Critical Links: Learning in the Arts and Student Academic and Social Development* and led the development of the AEP agenda for future arts education research, *The Arts and Education: New Opportunities for Research*. Prior to her work at AEP, she researched school reform and youth policy and trained youth advocates for the American Institutes for Research; founded and directed a performing arts and social change project in New York City; and was a policy, planning, and research associate with the President's Initiative on Race at the White House during the Clinton Administration. She owes great thanks to those who have taught her the arts, especially Margaret Axtell, Mary Lechter, and Percy Martin.

Acknowledgments

We are deeply indebted and grateful to the students, teachers, administrators, artists, and community members at the ten schools we studied to produce this book. Our debt and thanks are twofold: they allowed us into their lives and they spoke with candor and conviction about their schools. In return we promised them personal privacy, so we do not use their names, and we promised to tell their stories as honestly and accurately as we could. We hope we have done so.

At each of the schools, several staff members took on a number of burdens for us: arranging our visits, coordinating the participation of their schools in the several national meetings we convened during the study, providing the demographic and historical information in the school profiles, and reviewing the draft of the book for factual accuracy.

To the following we are grateful for these multiple contributions: Deanna Camputaro and Len Newman at Central Falls High School; Rebecca Hennis and Theresa Wuebbels at Clarkton School of Discovery; Roslyn Harris and Henry Walker at Dyett Academic Center High School; Diana Pasquini at Grizzly Hill School; Helen Schell, Mary Lou Schweikert, and Marissa Vickers at Hand Middle School; John Snavely and Jan Vesely at Peter Howell Elementary School; Gloria Doering, Sherri Pittard, and Julie Shepard at Newton D. Baker School of Arts; Deborah Davis and Lynne Mize at Pierce Street Elementary School; Joanna Hefferen and Margarita Nell at P.S. 130; and Bettine Hermanson, Roberta Puzon, and Mary Jo Thompson at Sheridan Global Arts and Communications School.

Serving on the teams of researchers who did the field work in the schools were Jose Colchado, Sheryl Cozart, Paula Groves-Price, Michael Gunzenhauser, Mark Hicks, Rob Horowitz, Terry Morris, George Noblit, Alejandra Velez-Paschke, and Anne Marie White. They brought a wealth of skill and experience to helping us collect and interpret our data.

Advice on the indicators of school success and research protocols used in the study came from researchers Terry Baker, James Catterall,

Allison Marshall, George Noblit, Steve Seidel, and Bruce Wilson. They helped us sharpen our tools for investigation.

A team of outstanding education administrators gave important guidance as the study unfolded, challenging us to present the study in a manner appealing not only to their colleagues but to a broader audience. We can only hope that Mary Cary, Jose Colchado, Yvonne Aguilera, and Paul Young feel we have succeeded.

Rob Horowitz and Bruce Wilson read early drafts of the book and advised on how to improve the presentation of our findings. Steve Seidel critiqued successive drafts and gave sensitive and specific guidance that made the book stronger and, we hope, more compelling to readers. For that and his very generous Foreword, words fail.

We are grateful to Brent Almond of Design Nut for his imagination and patience in designing the book and to Bob Howe and Art Halbrook for their copy editing.

Rebecca Borden and Andrew Nelson on the Arts Education Partnership staff, and consultant Denise Averbug, provided research assistance at various stages of the research and book production.

For generous financial support for the project we are immensely grateful to three major funders. The U.S. Congress appropriated funds specifically for the project, conveyed to us through a grant from the U.S. Department of Education. The GE Foundation continued its history of support for our research activities. Jean Collier, comptroller and program officer at the Foundation, provided the grant for this study and has been patient and steadfast in her support over its four year gestation. At the Ford Foundation, we owe much to Cyrus Driver and Margaret Wilkerson, not only for their financial support, but also for asking that we give special attention to the role of the arts in building community, a crucial focus that played a major role in shaping the interpretations and conclusions of the study.

The Geraldine R. Dodge Foundation has provided annual grants in recent years to support the daily operations of the Arts Education Partnership, permitting us to allocate the funding to meet our needs. Portions of the Dodge grants were dedicated to *Third Space* activities.

The Arts Education Partnership exists and has stayed on course for ten years thanks to the annual financial support of the National Endowment for the Arts and the U.S. Department of Education and the administrative support of the Council of Chief State School Officers and the National Assembly of State Arts Agencies. We are grateful to these organizations and specifically to the senior officials who represented them on the AEP Governance Committee throughout the study: Eileen Mason, Susan Sclafani, Tom Houlihan, and Jonathan Katz, respectively. We extend gratitude as well to our colleagues at the organizations that participate in the Arts Education Partnership, in particular to those serving on our Steering Committee, who continually deepen our understanding of the contexts and processes of the arts and education. We owe a debt as well to those researchers within the field of arts education and beyond who are illuminating the nature of, and necessary conditions for, effective teaching and learning and positive youth development. From them we have learned much and drawn liberally in interpreting and presenting the findings in *Third Space*.

For being constant sources of support, advice, and constructive criticism lovingly delivered, thanks to Kathleen Deasy and Frank Adamson.

Endnotes

PREFACE

1   National Commission on Excellence in Education. (1983). *A nation at risk: The imperative for educational reform.* Washington, DC: U.S. Department of Education (p. 5).

CHAPTER 1

2   Hannula, M. (2001). Third space: A merry-go-round of opportunity. *Kaisma Magazine, 12.* Retrieved on August 30, 2005 from http://www.kiasma.fi/www/viewresource.php?id= 3LoHln6PkQfTgv09&lang=en&preview=). See also M. Hannula (2000, May 25), *Misunderstandings as an ethical principle: A journey into third space.* Paper presented at the Momentum International Art Conference, Norway. Retrieved August 30, 2005 from http://kunst.no/questioning/old/mika.html.

In addition to its use in the arts, the metaphor of "third space" is also developing a place in educational research employing discourse analysis. In particular, Guttierez and colleagues at the University of California at Berkeley define "third space" as a space where students' "unofficial scripts" find authentic interaction with the "official scripts" of schools and teachers—a "social space within which counter-hegemonic activity, or contestation of dominant discourses, can occur for both students and teachers." [Gutierrez, K., Rimes, B., & J. Larson (1995). Script, counterscript, and underlife in the classroom: James Brown Versus Brown v. Board of Education. Harvard Educational Review. 65:3, 445-471]. Though we do not draw our analysis of third space from the body of work on the topic found in discourse analysis, our conceptualization of third space does resonate with it. Because we construe the third space opened in the arts as a learning environment for students that is not physical but rather composed of sets of relationships between and among students, artists, and teachers, this "space" may be seen as a discursive one.

3   Consortium of National Arts Education Associations. (2002). *Authentic connections: Interdisciplinary work in the arts.* Reston, VA: Consortium of National Arts Education Associations (pp. 3-10).

4   Booth, E. (2003). Seeking definition: What is a teaching artist? *Teaching Artist Journal. 1*(1). 5-12.

5   Dyett Academic also serves the middle grades but our research at the school focused on the high school level.

CHAPTER 2

6   Stipek, D., et al. (2004). *Engaging schools: Fostering high school students' motivation to learn.* Washington, DC: National Academies Press (p.28).

7   The National Research Council was organized by the National Academy of Sciences in 1916 to associate the broad community of science and technology with the Academy's purposes of furthering knowledge and advising the federal government.

8   Eccles, J., & Gootman, J. A. (Eds.). (2002). *Community programs to promote youth development*. Washington, DC: National Academy Press (p. 103).

9   Greene, M. (1995). *Releasing the imagination: Essays on education, the arts, and social change*. San Francisco: Jossey-Bass (pp. 32-43). See also M. Greene (1978), *Landscapes of learning*. New York: Teachers College Press (pp. 213-224) and M. Greene (1973), *Teacher as stranger*. Belmont, CA: Wadsworth (pp. 131-132).

10 Greene, p. 34.

11 Eisner, E. W. (2002). *The arts and the creation of mind*. New Haven, CT: Yale University Press (p. 3).

12 Eisner, p. 44.

13 Bransford, J., Brown, A. L., & Cocking, R. R. (Eds.).(1999). *How people learn: Brain, mind, experience, and school* (Expanded ed.). Washington, DC: National Academy Press (p. 61).

14 Since our visit to Newton D. Baker, it has expanded to serve students in pre-kindergarten through grade eight.

15 Benard, B. (2004). *Resiliency: What we have learned*. San Francisco: WestEd (pp. 47-48).

16 McLaughlin, M. W. (1993) Embedded identities. In S. B. Health and M. W. McLaughlin (Eds.) *Identity & inner-city youth: Beyond ethnicity and gender*. New York: Teachers College Press (p. 59).

17 Benard, p. 24.

CHAPTER 3

18 OECD DeSeCo Project. (2005). *The definition and selection of key competencies: Executive summary*. Paris, France: OECD. Retrieved on August 30, 2005 from https://www.pisa.oecd.org/dataoecd/47/61/35070367.pdf

19 Hannula, retrieved August 30, 2005 from http://www.kiasma.fi/www/viewresource.php?id =3LoHln6PkQfTgv09&lang=en&preview=).

20 Donovan, S. M., Bransford, J. D., and Pellegrino, J. W. (Eds.). (1999). *How people learn: Bridging research and practice*. Washington, DC: National Academy Press (p. 2).

21 Donovan, Bransford, & Pellegrino, p. 17.

22 The UCLA researcher James Catterall discusses the impact of this type of experience in his analysis of recent studies of drama in R. J. Deasy (Ed.). (2002), *Critical links: Learning in the arts and student academic and social development* (pp. 58-62). He writes: "Getting out of role to direct, suggest, and/or discuss aspects of what is transpiring during a dramatic portrayal ... are indicative of meta-cognitive activities and are evidence of engagement and concentrated thought."

23 Wolf, D. P. (2000). Why the arts matter in education or just what do children learn when they create an opera? In E. Fiske (Ed.), *Champions of change: The impact of arts on learning.* Washington, DC: Arts Education Partnership and the President's Committee on the Arts and the Humanities (p. 98).

24 Swartz, D. L., Bransford, J. D., & Sears, D. (2005). Efficiency and innovation in transfer. In J. P. Mestre (Ed.), *Transfer of learning from a modern multidisciplinary perspective.* Greenwich, CT: Information Age Publishing (pp. 27-32).

25 Swartz, Bransford, & Sears, pp. 37-41.

26 Swartz, Bransford, & Sears, p. 42.

27 Eisner, p. 7.

28 Eisner, p. 206.

29 Papert, S. (2002, August, 24). How to make writing 'hard fun.' *Bangor Daily News.* p. A7. Retrieved August 26, 2005, from http://www.papert.org/articles/HardFun.html. Italics original.

30 Bransford, Brown, & Cocking

31 McLaughlin, pp. 36-69.

32 Stipek et al. pp. 44-54.

33 Stipek, et al., pp. 49-52.

CHAPTER 4

34 Au, K. H. (1993). *Literacy instruction in multicultural settings.* Orlando, FL: Harcourt-Brace College Press (pp. 33-34).

CHAPTER 5

35 Benard, p. 74.

36 Donovan, Bransford, & Pellegrino, p. 10.

37 Donovan, Bransford, & Pellegrino, p. 19.

38 Corbett, D., Wilson, B, & Williams, B. (2002). *Effort and excellence in urban classrooms: Expecting, and getting, success with all students.* New York: Teachers College Press.

39 Ingersoll, R. M., & Smith, T. M. (2003). The wrong solution to the teacher shortage. *Educational Leadership. 60*(8), 30-33. See also Smith, T. M. & Ingersoll, R. M. (2004), What are the effects of induction and mentoring in beginning teacher turnover? *American Educational Research Journal, 41*(3), 681-714.

40 Oreck, B. (2004). The artistic and professional development of teachers: A study of teachers' attitudes toward and use of the arts in teaching. *Journal of Teacher Education, 55*(1), 55-69.

41 Oreck, pp. 59-64.

42 Swartz, Bransford, & Sears, pp. 1-51.

43 Benard, p. 74.

44 Greene, p. 36.

45 Greene, p. 14.

CHAPTER 6

46 Sergiovanni, T. (1994). *Building community in schools.* San Francisco, CA: Jossey-Bass (p. xi).

47 Barton, P. E. (2005). *One-third of a nation: Rising dropout rates and declining opportunities.* Princeton, NJ: Educational Testing Service (p. 7).

48 Greene, J., & Winters, M. (2005). Public high school graduation and college-readiness rates: 1991–2002. *Education working paper 8.* New York: Manhattan Institute. Retrieved August 30, 2005 from http://www.manhattan-institute.org/html/ewp_08.htm.

49 Ingersoll & Smith, p. 30-33.

50 Sergiovanni, p. 124.

51 Sergiovanni, p. 122.

52 Sergiovanni, p. 123.

53 Educational researcher James S. Catterall links the development of empathy, tolerance and moral reasoning to experiences in the arts. For additional information see Catterall, J. S. (1995). Involvement in the arts and human development: General involvement and intensive involvement in music and theater arts. In E. B. Fiske (Ed.), *Champions of change: The impact of arts on learning.* (pp.1-19). Washington, DC: Arts Education Partnership and the President's Committee on the Arts and the Humanities.

54 Greene, p. 36.

55 Carrillo, R. (2000). Intersections of official script and learner script in third space: A case study of Latino families in an afterschool computer program. In B. Fishman & S. O'Connor-Divelbiss (Eds.), *Fourth international conference of the learning sciences.* Mahwah, NJ: Erlbaum.

References

Arts Education Partnership. (2004). *The arts and education: New opportunities for research.* Washington, DC: Arts Education Partnership.

Au, K. H. (1993). *Literacy instruction in multicultural settings.* Orlando, FL: Harcourt-Brace College Press.

Barton, P. E. (2005). *One-third of a nation: Rising dropout rates and declining opportunities.* Princeton, NJ: Educational Testing Service.

Benard, B. (2004). *Resiliency: What we have learned.* San Francisco: WestEd.

Boyer, E. L. (1995). *The basic school: A community for learning.* Princeton, NJ: Carnegie Foundation for the Advancement of Teaching.

Booth, E. (2003). Seeking definition: What is a teaching artist? *Teaching Artist Journal. 1*(1). 5-12.

Bransford, J., Brown, A. L., & Cocking, R. R. (Eds.). (1999). *How people learn: Brain, mind, experience, and school* (Expanded ed.). Washington, DC: National Academy Press.

Bransford, J., & Swartz, A. (1999). Rethinking transfer: A simple proposal with educational implications. *Review of Research in Education, 24.*

Brookover, W. (1978). Elementary school climate and school achievement. *American Educational Research Journal, 15,* 301-308.

Carrillo, R. (2000). Intersections of official script and learner script in third space: A case study of Latino families in an afterschool computer program. In B. Fishman & S. O'Connor-Divelbiss (Eds.), *Fourth international conference of the learning sciences.* Mahwah, NJ: Erlbaum.

Catterall, J. S. (1995). Involvement in the arts and human development: General involvement and intensive involvement in music and theater arts. In E. B. Fiske (Ed.), *Champions of change: The impact of arts on learning.* (pp.1-19). Washington, DC: Arts Education Partnership and the President's Committee on the Arts and the Humanities.

Catterall, J. S. (2002). The arts and the transfer of learning. In R. J. Deasy (Ed.), *Critical links: Learning in the arts and student academic and social development* (pp. 151-157). Washington, DC: Arts Education Partnership.

Catterall, J. S. (2002). Research on drama and theater in education. In R. J. Deasy (Ed.), *Critical links: Learning in the arts and student academic and social development* (pp. 58-62). Washington, DC: Arts Education Partnership.

Consortium of National Arts Education Associations. (2002). *Authentic connections: Interdisciplinary work in the arts.* Reston, VA: Consortium of National Arts Education Associations.

Corbett, D., et al. (2001). *The arts, school identity, and comprehensive education reform: A final report from the evaluation of the A+ schools program*. Winston-Salem, NC: Thomas S. Kenan Institute for the Arts.

Corbett, D., Wilson, B, & Williams, B. (2002). *Effort and excellence in urban classrooms: Expecting, and getting, success with all students*. New York: Teachers College Press.

Deasy, R. J. (Ed.). (2002). *Critical links: Learning in the arts and student academic and social development*. Washington, DC: Arts Education Partnership.

Dewey. J. (1959). *Art as experience*. New York: Perigree Trade

Donovan, S. M., Bransford, J. D., & Pellegrino, J. W. (Eds.). (1999). *How people learn: Bridging research and practice*. Washington, DC: National Academies Press.

Eccles, J., & Gootman, J. A. (Eds.). (2002). *Community programs to promote youth development*. Washington, DC: National Academy Press.

Eisner, E. W. (2002). *The arts and the creation of mind*. New Haven, CT: Yale University Press.

Fiske, E. (Ed). (1995). *Champions of change: The impact of arts on learning*. Washington, DC: Arts Education Partnership and the President's Committee on the Arts and the Humanities.

Goldhawk, S. (1998). *Young children and the arts: Making creative connections*. Washington, DC: Arts Education Partnership.

Greene, J., & Winters, M. (2005). Public high school graduation and college-readiness rates: 1991–2002. *Education Working Paper 8*. New York: Manhattan Institute. Retrieved August 30, 2005 from http://www.manhattan-institute.org/html/ewp_08.htm.

Greene, M. (1973). *Teacher as stranger*. Belmont, CA: Wadsworth.

Greene, M. (1978). *Landscapes of learning*. New York: Teachers College Press.

Greene, M. (1995). *Releasing the imagination: Essays on education, art and social change*. San Francisco: Jossey-Bass.

Gutman, A. (1987). *Democratic education*. Princeton, NJ: Princeton University Press.

Hannula, M. (2001). Third space: A merry-go-round of opportunity. *Kaisma Magazine, 12*. Retrieved August 30, 2005 from http://www.kiasma.fi/www/viewresource.php?id=3Lo HIn6PkQfTgv09&lang=en&preview=)

Hannula, M. (2000, May). *Misunderstandings as an ethical principle: A journey into third space*. Paper presented at the Momentum International Art Conference, Norway. Retrieved August 30, 2005 from http://kunst.no/questioning/old/mika.html

Heath, S. B. (2001). Three's not a crowd: Plans, roles and focus in the arts. *Educational Researcher, 30*(7), 10-17.

Heath, S. B., & Smyth, L. (1999). *ArtShow: Youth and community development—A resource guide*. Washington, DC: Partners for Livable Communities.